ASK AN ADVENTURER

Behind the scenes: making a living from
living adventurously, growing an audience,
and unconventional creativity.

ALASTAIR HUMPHREYS

CONTENTS

Behind the Scenes   7

The Working Adventurer   13

Money   23

Time   57

Writing   75

Speaking   97

Social Media   115

Connecting   135

General Questions   155

*Tempora mutantur, nos et
mutamur in illis.*

Times are changed, we also are
changed with them.

I'm sure like a lot of you
People often ask me what do you do
To which I reply, 'I rap'
To which they reply, 'Yeah, but besides that'
To which I reply, 'Not much'
To which they reply with awkward coughs and such
Until I feel compelled to elaborate
This is not a hobby
Do it for my salary mate
And been doing so for well over a decade
See I get paid for putting pen to page
Performing sets on stage
And when selectas play my record
Let's just say that at the end of the day
That's how I collect my wage

At which point they inevitably say
'Damn, that's how you're expenses are paid?'
Yes, that's what I'm attempting to say
'Well that's great getting to do what you love every day'
And yes, it may seem like I'm living the dream
But hey there's much more to it when you go behind the scenes.

– 'Behind the Scenes' from Still Hungry by DJ Format and Abdominal

BEHIND THE SCENES

Many years ago, I heard a woman on Radio 4 describe herself as a 'working artist'. I didn't catch her name, but the interview struck a chord with me. She regarded her art as more than just a hobby, a passion or an identity: it was also her job. She was not embarrassed about calling the thing she loved 'work' and did not consider that earning money demeaned her art. She loved what she did, and she also made it pay the bills.

The phrase 'working artist' neatly encapsulated my own hopes and fears. I loved adventure, but could it be my job too? Would I fall out of love with adventure if I had to think about it every day and use it to earn money? Could I harness the idealistic, whimsical musings that drifted gently around my mind like campfire smoke when I was out in wild places and turn them into cold, hard cash? Dough, dosh, moolah, wonga. Could I become comfortable with self-promotion and showing off about myself? Why didn't I get a regular job and just go on adventures in my holidays? On the other hand, the prospect of being my own boss, in charge of my own destiny, going to incredible places and calling it all 'work' sounded like winning the lottery.

I have been obsessed with adventure for a quarter of a century and working at it full-time for the best part of 20 years. Accompanying many adventures have been 13 books, scores of short films and podcasts, a couple of thousand blog posts and a thousand or more talks and keynote presentations. I have shared ideas on living adventurously with companies like Google, HSBC, Facebook, Amazon and Virgin Galactic. I have worked on campaigns about adventure with brands including Land Rover, Glenfiddich, Adidas, Visit Britain and Cartier. I even bagged an amusing cameo role as 'Alastair Humphreys, adventurer' in a cider advert on TV.

I have given talks on six continents to audiences as large as 1600 and as low as zero (don't ask), and as diverse as toddlers, pensioners and Special Forces soldiers. My favourite part is always the Q&A session at the end, although the same questions do crop up time and again (*What's your favourite country? Wasn't it dangerous?*). Generally, people ask about the journeys I have been on and what they have taught me. The joyous exception to this rule are the random questions young children ask. (*Is your favourite colour blue? What's for lunch? Where do you go to the toilet? My mummy has got a bike.*) I get asked all sorts of questions about the practical, emotional, physical and mental aspects of getting from A to B in wild places. It is very rare these days to hear a question I have never heard before. I love novel questions because they force me into thinking mode rather than the autopilot I occasionally lapse into (*Do you have a boyfriend, and if not, are you busy tonight?*).

Yet whilst adventures are the most colourful part of my life, I don't spend all my time away on journeys. Although my career revolves around outdoor travel, I actually spend more time wading through emails than swimming in rivers. Yet nobody ever asks about what goes on behind the scenes of a Working Adventurer's life. That is what this book is about.

Being an adventurer is like being back at school. Some kids were good at sport, some shone in the classroom, and others were popular. (And then there was me, but that's a conversation for another day, or a therapist.) There were awards for academia (nobody cared much about those) and the sports champions received both trophies (more prestigious) and adulation. Then there were the cool kids, popular without ever seeming to do much because they were funny, charming or attractive. Everyone scrabbled to find their niche. Life is much the same in the adventure world.

You find athletes making their mark with bold expeditions, clever folk writing masterpieces or championing conservation work and those who get along through charisma or good looks. Every Working Adventurer tackles life in their own way.

This book is about what *my* life has been like as a Working Adventurer. I make no claim to it being a definitive handbook. It is not a book championing elite performance or stellar success, nor a guide to being the best of the best, filled with hacks to help you seek marginal gains and crush the opposition. I'm not that sort of person. I will never be as tough as Ranulph Fiennes, as famous and wealthy as Bear Grylls or sell as many books as any number of writers. I'm not the 'best' adventurer out there.

I am under no illusion of being amongst the outliers in my field, those who are the most extreme, productive, well-known or wealthy. Then again, I'm pretty sure the artist I heard on the radio was not as talented or renowned as Frida Kahlo or Picasso, but she was doing what she loved and earning a living from it. That felt like success to me. Picasso, on the other hand, had loftier ideas for the working artist. 'What are the aims of the artist?' he asked. 'Fame, money and beautiful lovers.'

There are many ways to build a life. This book is how I do things, but it's not the way you should do them. I am sure other Working Adventurers would disagree with a lot of it and offer other advice in its place. I have merely tried to be honest about the way I work. What I don't do in these pages is answer the usual questions I get asked. There are no kit lists, no practical expedition planning advice, no daring deeds. I have written other books about all that. Here, I simply show you the bodged-together set design of a Working Adventurer's visible facade.

I felt it was important to counter the Instagram glossiness of not only my online life, but the prevalence of seemingly perfect, envy-inducing online lives in general. It is not healthy to see so much curated polish. I wanted to lift the curtain and invite you backstage to see the reality of the mess that I usually shove hastily into the wings, out of sight.

The book's genesis was an awareness that the questions I answer in my talks and the stories I share on stage and social media are just the tip of the iceberg of my working life. Kayaking amongst bright blue icebergs is one thing. But who does my tax returns? And what do I do all day in my shed other than drink coffee and look out of the window at the birds?

Away from the visible face of adventures, what has it been like to build a life and a living from adventure? How did I get started and build momentum? I explain how I gathered the nerve to leap from being a salaried teacher to self-employment. I share practical details about my daily working routine, getting published, launching a podcast, or starting earning money from public speaking. I explain how I make money (and how much I earn), address how I get the time for adventures amidst family life and explore whether adventure isn't entirely pointless and self-indulgent. And I tackle some general interest questions which I enjoyed reflecting on.

I hope you will enjoy this book if you love everything about adventure. It may also appeal if you just like a good rummage through someone's drawers. Some aspects might overlap with your own life, whether that is attempting to live adventurously amidst the hectic rush of daily life, daring yourself to go freelance in a creative industry or considering carving a career from something you love.

I enjoy the Q&A sessions in my talks because it is a chance for the audience to ask what *they* are interested in, not what I've chosen to bang on about. I took the same approach here and invited questions about being a Working Adventurer via social media. I received hundreds of questions, convincing me that there were enough nosey but nice folk interested in the illusionist's techniques of my life to give this book a go. (You can ask questions here in case Part 2 ever materialises: www.bit.ly/AskAnAdventurer.)

When I began, I was uncertain what direction it might take. It depended on what questions people asked me. But in the same way that serendipity, momentum and adventure show up once you dare yourself to get out of the front door and have a look around, I decided just to give it a go.

Every week I picked a question from the growing list, climbed onto my bike and went for a ride to mull it over. Then I'd find a café, order lunch and scribble down my thoughts. It was a satisfying way to write a book. If cycling helped Einstein come up with the theory of relativity ('I thought of that whilst riding my bicycle,' he supposedly said), then it was certainly good enough for me...

THE WORKING ADVENTURER

What on earth is an 'adventurer'?

My short definition of a Working Adventurer is someone who earns money from their adventures as opposed to someone who enjoys adventure as a hobby or takes a break from work to go travelling. But an 'explorer' or an 'extreme athlete' could also do that. What is the difference?

Calling yourself an 'explorer' certainly sounds impressive. Everyone has an idea of what an explorer is. If you can pull it off, then I can think of no finer business card. But I am not an explorer, sadly. I've never been somewhere that hasn't been mapped. I've never discovered anything new, let alone anything that is both new and useful. I believe that an explorer needs to return home with knowledge. There are also old-fashioned connotations of the word that don't feel appropriate for what I do. I don't wear a pith helmet.

If you Google 'adventurer', you'll find 76 million pages beginning with a bunch of dictionary definitions, and then comes an article by me! Compare that with twenty times as many pages about explorers. Even removing those linked to Microsoft Explorer or the Ford Explorer only culls a tenth of the entries. That these companies have hijacked the explorer word and image makes it feel even less suitable for my own life.

'Adventurer' is a vague term that depends upon the root word 'adventure'. I have always been adamant that everyone's definition of adventure can be different. One person's little jaunt is another's Everest. Someone else's Everest is another's vanity project. Yet if I leave it up to you to define adventure it doesn't make it easy for me to explain 'adventurer'. So here is my take on it.

To my mind, being an adventurer is linked with the experiences you have along the way more than the lands you conquer. It feels like a 21st-Century term, an excitement-seeking soul rather than a serious fellow with a patron or independent means. Being an adventurer feels accessible to more people and free from stigma, dogma, or restrictions of elitism or gender. It is possible to be both an average person and an adventurer. An adventurer belongs in our era of social media, story-telling, enjoyable journeys and challenges, rather than the days of Columbus or Shackleton. The worst of what adventurers do is an exercise in vanity, chasing a scrolling, envious audience. At best, an adventurer makes people smile, challenges them to think, brings about change and inspires action.

How else might I describe myself if not as an adventurer? Dispelling some other titles might counter any illusions you might have that a Working Adventurer is somehow exceptionally talented, skilled or qualified in a way that you are not.

- Athlete? I have run marathons and an ultramarathon or two, but I certainly am not an athlete. I have never won a race, and I am happy to swap running for tree climbing if I get the chance.
- Traveller? Romantically appealing, yes. But I have spent the past decade championing the merits of *not* needing to go on long, meandering journeys in order to live adventurously. It is also liable to be confused with other traditionally itinerant groups.
- Microadventurer? This, perhaps, is the best description for most of my life at the moment, but it is an ugly word, and you first need to establish what 'adventurer' means anyway.
- Writer? I would love this to be the one-word summary of my life, but imposter syndrome and income percentage deter me.
- Motivational Speaker? I enjoy giving talks; I have been doing it for

many years; it feels worthwhile, and it pays most of my bills. But it also feels like a job description rather than a life description, and not one I particularly aspire to.

- Film-maker / podcaster? I like making films, but I'm only a dabbler. I'm enthusiastic about podcasts, but I've only been doing it a short while. I cannot claim to be defined by either of those.
- Social Media Influencer? *Wipes vomit from floor...*

Perhaps being an adventurer is about the difference between being a jack-of-all-trades versus being a specialist. 'Jack vs The Specialist' is the title of a long-running email discussion I've been having with climber Paul Deegan over many years.

Back when explorer Ben Saunders and I were working on a South Pole expedition, he would berate me for spreading myself too thin and trying to do a little bit of everything, rather than just doing one thing well. I took Ben's point, but I just can't help dashing off like a puppy to investigate all the different, delightful smells and adventures in the woods. Ben is a focused explorer. I am a dilettante adventurer. All I am interested in is everything, 'desirous of everything at the same time'. With this comes an acceptance that in its place I must forfeit the chance to be the best at anything: I will never be an 'explorer' or an 'athlete' or a great 'writer' without narrowing my focus. And I am OK with that.

Whatever I decide to call myself, the work aspect of all this adventure stuff only occupies a mere 30 hours out of my week's 168 hours anyway. The majority of my time, I am just 'Dad', picking my kids up from school and cooking tea for the family. A crucial part of my personal definition of being an adventurer is that its essence ought to run right through all those other hours in a way that it might not if I was a butcher, a baker or a candlestick maker. This is more than my job. It is my life.

I don't want to think in terms of adventure or work, adventure or downtime, adventure or family. I want my life to be adventure and work, adventure and downtime, adventure and family. To build my life around the intangible essence of all that being an adventurer implies.

My choice of the word 'adventurer' is a statement of intent to myself, a reminder to be curious, enthusiastic and as bold as I dare to be at all hours, not just those when I've clocked on for work.

'Adventurer' might be a clunky label of convenience, but it clarifies that I am not an explorer nor an accountant. It goes some way towards encapsulating my passion, my income and my lifestyle priorities. I have no other job or hidden wealth. As a Working Adventurer, I pay my bills solely via the adventures I go on and the stories I tell afterwards.

IF YOU WEREN'T AN ADVENTURER, WHAT WOULD YOU WANT TO BE?

What I'd *want* to be is a professional sportsman. What I'd *actually* have been is a teacher.

When did you decide that you were an adventurer?

During the four years when I was cycling around the world and genuinely having an adventure every single day, I did not think of myself as an adventurer. I was just a young man on a long bike ride. I do remember the distinctive nuances between the words 'tourist', 'backpacker' and 'traveller' amongst the people I met along the way. So I guess that names and labels have always mattered, vague and blurry though they may be.

Somewhere back then, I enjoyed the book *Are You Experienced*, a novel about backpackers versus tourists, though I suspect it may not have aged well. I liked the quote, 'There was a general belief that a long and unpleasant holiday was of crucial importance to one's development as a human being.'

The Beach resonated with me too at that time: 'If I'd learnt one thing from travelling, it was that the way to get things done was to go ahead and do them. Don't talk about going to Borneo. Book a ticket, get a visa, pack a bag and it just happens.'

I still did not feel like an adventurer after cycling around the world, but I had, at last, done a big adventure and felt closer to belonging to the club. Did I deem myself more of an adventurer after my next big trip? Did I think it after getting paid to do a talk? After publishing a book? Or was it when I quit being a teacher and committed to trying to make it my full-time job?

That probably was the point when I began committing to the moniker, which confirms my earlier definition that a Working Adventurer is someone who earns money from their escapades and has the temerity to claim that such a ludicrous tag is actually their profession.

DO YOU SUFFER FROM IMPOSTER SYNDROME AND, IF SO, HOW DO YOU TACKLE IT?

I still feel a fraud when someone introduces me as an 'adventurer'. I feel undeserving when in the company of those who have completed more significant challenges than me, and I feel uneasy answering all these questions with a seemingly authoritative air.

Practice and experience are the best way to tackle imposter syndrome. Over time, you learn that everyone else is winging it too. I read something once about Barrack Obama feeling out of his depth when he became President. And if Obama does not have his act together, then clearly none of us do.

How has the world of adventure changed since you started?

The world of adventure has changed a great deal since my first big journey 25 years ago, heading off nervously with a big rucksack to spend a year in Africa.

Above all, the adventure world has opened up massively. This is wonderful. You, the reader, will come from a much more diverse audience, with a far wider interpretation of 'adventure' than when I began devouring travel books in the 1990s.

In those days, there was a segregated hierarchy of a few near-mythic heroes doing exotic expeditions, and then there was the rest of us reading about them. Those adventures were primarily the domain of people (mostly men) who were tough, well-connected or able to fund themselves.

Adventure used to be very niche and not something that registered with 'normal' folk. Today adventure has become fashionable and mainstream. Glossy magazines like Sidetracked showcase beautiful people doing awesome journeys in breathtaking locations. Photography and style have become integral parts of many adventures. Adventure often looks enviable rather than a brutal suffer-fest. The North Face brand (who recently teamed up with Gucci for a marketing campaign that included a £400 sunhat) has ambassadors ranging from genuinely world-class climbers to a 'network of restless explorers – from wave makers to groundbreakers – united by a belief that we can and should do better'. These 'explorers' include DJs and dancers. Adventure is not just the domain of professional tough guys anymore. Large numbers of ordinary people are getting involved in the outdoors. That makes me happy. Adventure should be democratised and accessible to all.

There is still a place in my heart for the glory of horizon-busting, daredevil adventure. But I am delighted that an adventurous soul stuck in a stifling city office now feels that a weekend escapade is for them as well.

In terms of getting involved, there is a much broader range of activities available today. It's not just scaling mountains, trekking to poles or crossing oceans and continents, but stand up paddleboarding and urban adventure races as well.

The number, and the range, of participants has also grown considerably. Adventure used to appeal to men with beards wearing smelly Ron Hill Tracksters. Now it is a word and a concept widely embraced by athletes and artists, poets and paragliders, running mums and retired enthusiasts, not to mention so many different brands. There are far more women involved in adventure than used to be the case. Adventure has expanded from pursuing experiences in the Himalayas or Highlands to a much more inclusive, everyday vibe. (Dare I mention the word 'microadventure'?) Huge numbers of us now enjoy participating in outdoor sports, adventure races, expeditions or exotic travels. We do it at every possible level, from ParkRuns to winter ascents of K2.

Reflecting on my lasting love of all things adventurous, I recognise how much I have changed too. That is not surprising; I have grown up and grown old (or at least middle-aged) in the company of wild places and people. I used to be obsessed with epic, masochistic feats. I read every travel and adventure book I could get my hands on; the madder the journey, the better. Over time I have perhaps drunk my fill of that. I have become more interested in nature and tales of those who stay in one place and drink deeply of their adventurous experiences there. I have begun to feel greater pulls in new creative directions, to take stock, ask more questions, listen more and pay closer attention.

For even longer than I have relished crossing remote landscapes or negotiating crazy foreign cities, I have loved the stories of adventures. It was reading books that first filled my head with exuberant and exotic ideas. So adventure story-telling has always been a key aspect of not only the journeys I have been on, but also my attempts to become a Working Adventurer.

When I started travelling and writing at the end of the nineties, it was very much a fringe activity. Accounts of adventure were limited to just a few magazines and traditionally published books, with all of their gatekeepers standing in the way. It was a hard scrabble to get your writing published anywhere. Getting on TV or the radio felt impossible. Fast forward to today, and anyone can post a story on their internet streams, whether that is writing, photography, film or audio. There are now far more blogs, magazines, podcasts, festivals, exhibitions and speaking events than I could ever have imagined.

Despite that, it seems that the lament of travel writing being dead has been around for years. It was decades ago that Susan Sontag called travel writing the 'literature of disappointment'. Today anyone can travel anywhere, but not everyone can write about it well. Since I began writing blogs and books, I have noticed a broadening and a dilution of what is published. Yet the saturation of the adventure market also means that it is even more challenging for writers to get their books accepted by mainstream publishers.

But the revolution in self-publishing has also made it easier for us to get our stories out and find a small but interested audience. The gates have been flung open. More people can now take their place in the world of adventure and have a crack at earning a living from it.

Consequently, it is easier than ever to become a Working Adventurer, find your niche on the internet, build a tribe that is interested in what you do, and begin to monetise it. Yet this also means that in terms of earning potential and audience reach, the distinction between a full-time mountaineer and a full-time adventurous social media influencer has blurred to almost nothing. The sector has become ultra-competitive for attention as well as income. It will be interesting to see what implications unfurl for the Working Adventurer out of all this over the coming years.

Adventurous story-telling today includes the Outdoor Swimming Society, Intrepid magazine championing women in adventure, the Adventurous Ink book club for outdoor folk and all the everyday feats and triumphs of thousands of happy adventurers told through their Instagram pages.

WHAT IS YOUR FAVOURITE TIME OF DAY TO START A JOURNEY?

My favourite time to get going is always 30 minutes before first light.

MONEY

How do you earn enough money from adventure to make it a full-time job?

I could have earned a living from adventure in many different ways. But whatever route I plumped for, three things would have remained constant: the amount of time it requires to build momentum, an obsessive streak and a plan for surviving in the beginning.

To get going, I saved £7000 over five years through working a couple of part-time jobs. This money funded me cycling around the world with the help of some extreme parsimony. I never bought chocolate or treats. I never splashed out on fizzy drinks or a bottle of water, even in roasting temperatures. I made do with tepid tap water purified with iodine. Even when I was exhausted or afraid, I would always try to camp rather than pay for accommodation. If you can travel far or travel in style, always choose the long road.

Later, before I quit my proper teaching job to focus on adventure, I was already giving talks in my spare time. The headteacher once even let me miss a morning's school to give a talk, which is ludicrous when I think about it! I worked hard to build up my number of bookings. I sent so many emails chasing leads and succeeded with very few, developing a thick skin along the way. I dabbled with every social media fad to find my voice. I volunteered to speak at every adventure event I could find. I churned out blog posts.

I wrote my second book whilst still teaching. I squeezed writing in around the margins of my days, scribbling for ten minutes here and there in the staff room and pulling the occasional exhausting but exhilarating all-nighter. I needed to get to a point where I would still have enough money coming in to keep me afloat when I gave up my salary.

Eventually, I handed in my notice, giving up my pension and my union rep. Yet when I woke up on that first Monday morning to live as a self-employed, self-proclaimed Working Adventurer, I was not beginning from a standing start. I had 46,000 miles of stories, words and photographs under my belt. I had self-published a book and taken a night-school photography course. I was already in motion.

Since then, I have earned money in many different ways. First, let me clarify that this is how *I* make money, not how *you* should earn money. I'm not a financial expert, nor am I very savvy about money. Consider this a curious snoop into my desk drawers rather than expert strategies to follow. The only advice I would offer is that if you want enough cash to go on adventures, find a well-paying job with plenty of time off to go and climb your mountains. If you want to earn money out of expeditions directly, make it your first priority to save up money from a normal job and tackle a massive adventure with zero regard for earning money out of it. And if you want to get paid to spend as much time as possible in wild places, become an outdoor instructor, a mountain guide, a research scientist, a soldier or get a job that posts you overseas.

Two markers tend to separate those who make long careers from adventure from those who fall by the wayside: solving the dilemma of earning enough money and having the patience to plug away at it all for the long term.

Here is how I currently earn money:

- Affiliate marketing – This means earning a commission from promoting products online. I nearly always forget to set it up when recommending books or equipment. Consequently, it only brings in about a pound a day.
- Books – Although only an optimist or a celebrity would sit down to write a book for money, books are a useful way to bring in a steady

trickle throughout my life. I will also earn royalties on my books for 70 years after my death, when the copyrights expire. After that, my masterpieces will become available for pennies in knock-off editions with thin paper and lodes of typoes. To date, I have published 13 books in a variety of formats. These include:

- Audible – Eight of my books are available as audiobooks, a format growing in popularity. They are an easy way to reach a broad audience, being available to anyone globally and cheap to produce.
- Kindle – Most of my books are available on Kindle. It's an option that essentially costs nothing to provide but again opens you up to a wider readership.
- Paper versions – Frustratingly, my books are seldom stocked in bookshops for reasons including ineffective marketing by publishers, choosing to publish some books independently, lack of fame, competition and – of course – not being good enough to be selected for shelf space. Therefore Amazon and my online shop are key to my sales. I used to flog books out of my rucksack after talks then sprint to catch the last train home.

  Because I get a 50% discount from the publisher, selling books on my website has the best profit margin. It also entails more hassle than simply receiving a royalty cheque twice a year, as I do for all the other books I sell. For many years, I handled all orders myself, keeping stashes of books under the bed, signing every copy and taking them to the Post Office. It was a helpful way of building rapport with my customers. I have since outsourced the process to a social enterprise (Enabled Works) owned and run by its disabled workforce. All my other book sales, from websites and bookshops, are taken care of by my publishers.
- Brand ambassador programmes – I partner with brands over periods of a year or more to use their equipment, provide insights into its performance, attend events on their behalf and help promote the brand. In my early days, I was remunerated through free equipment before moving on to being paid.
- Brand campaigns – Working with a company to help promote and market a product is usually fantastic, but occasionally there can be a wee bit of feeling, 'Oh well, this makes me cringe a bit, but at least it's work.' These jobs tend to be the most significant lump sum

payments I receive, in healthy four- or five-figure sums.

- Brand films – I began making films just for fun. I never imagined it would lead to filming online adverts for companies, but this has become a decent income stream and one of my favourite aspects of work. Sometimes I work alone on films. On other occasions, they are an opportunity to get out of my shed and collaborate with friends or new and interesting people. They are time-consuming but well-paid projects.

- Kofi.com/al_humphreys – This is a way for readers to buy me a 'virtual coffee' if they enjoy a blog post or newsletter. Imagine it like a digital tip jar. Audiences are growing more comfortable with tipping for quality, free online content. I currently earn roughly £5 a day from Kofi.

- Magazine articles – The first time I got paid to write an article, after a year of cycling through Africa, I was so proud and amazed that I could get cash for writing about adventure. I sought out opportunities to write articles as not only do you get paid, it is also a way to reach a new audience and showcase your writing.

- Podcast sponsorship – I sell advertising space on my podcast, either per series or per episode.

- Photography – When I started out, I stuck my fingers in as many pies as possible. I uploaded some travel photos to a website selling greeting cards and suchlike. I can never be bothered to close the website down, and I only include this on the list because it still earns about £100 annually, almost 15 years later. That won't keep me in caviar, but the total it has made over the years is a small example of the cumulative benefits of passive income. It was certainly worth the couple of hours of initial work.

- Talks (corporate) – I give keynote presentations to businesses about the expeditions I have been on and the lessons gleaned along the way. Corporate events make up most of my speaking work today for the pragmatic (if not noble) reason that I don't have as much time as I used to and they pay ten times better than schools. My fees have crept up over the years, as you'd expect when your skills develop. I usually earn a few thousand pounds per event, nudging now and again into five figures, which sounds absurd for showing my holiday snaps and telling silly stories. It is reassuring to know that I am providing something fair when companies book me for repeat events.

- Talks (events) – Speaking at book festivals or adventure exhibitions can be fun, a chance to raise your profile and sell some books, but they generally pay terribly.
- Talks (schools) – Visiting schools to talk about adventure, the kindness of the world, dreaming big and starting small has been the longest, steadiest income of my life. It reassures me that there are a virtually unlimited number of schools to present at, with an ever-changing roster of pupils. If all my other ventures fail, this should remain a steady option for me, earning several hundred pounds or a low four-figures per event.

There are some typical Working Adventurer money-earning activities that I don't do, for various reasons: guiding, leading trips, writing guidebooks, TV, practical workshops, building hiking trails, online courses and paid newsletters. There are also some avenues that I've tried but stopped doing. These include:

- Blog advertising – back in the glory days of blogging, I earned a few grand a year from running adverts on my website. No longer, alas.
- Busking – I once lived for a month off the 120 Euros I earned playing my violin in Spain on a journey that led to me writing *My Midsummer Morning*.
- Corporate microadventures – People often contact me asking if I'll take them on a microadventure. Businesses are always on the lookout for interesting bonding projects for their staff. I also know the benefits of sitting round a campfire to sort out life's conundrums. So taking small groups out for the night seemed like a logical idea (and I still think it is a good one.) But it felt weird charging to sleep on a hill. It needed to be expensive to be worth bothering with, which clashed with my claims that adventure is for everyone. Plus, it was all a bit of a hassle to arrange. Therefore after a few experiments with good food, beautiful landscapes and honest, challenging conversation, I shelved the idea. It was a pity as the events had been successful.

  Had I been so inclined, I'm sure this could have become a full-time occupation. However, it is fair to say that a few keyboard warriors got irate at my experiment in earning money from microadventures. (It's worth pointing out that people often get miffed at the idea of making money from adventure, but they tend not to offer alternative suggestions for getting paid.)

- Expedition advice – One of the constant wars of my life (and yours, I suspect) is against the tyranny of email and the license it gives others to make demands on your time with little effort on their part (and no intention to cause you problems). So many people emailed me for expedition planning advice beyond the articles and books I had already written that I experimented with charging for Skype calls to help plan expeditions. In reality, whenever anyone was actually willing to pay to talk to me, I felt so honoured and guilty that I then just called them for free. So I made zero money from this, but it did act as a good filter for finding individuals who were serious about their plans and respected my time enough to consider paying. I was happy to help them without charging.
- Magazine columns – I wrote a monthly column for Trail magazine for a year. I enjoyed it, but stopping doing it freed up a lot of mental bandwidth, time and enthusiasm to focus my writing efforts on books. It is increasingly hard to make a living from paid freelance writing, but I used to love the thrill of seeing my own words and photos in print magazines and newspapers.
- School worksheets – I did a little freelance work for a charity, creating educational worksheets based on my bike trip round the world.
- Selling #microadventure t-shirts – Let's just say that there are many headaches involved when you bulk order stock, have loads of colour options and sizes and have to deal with all the orders, shipping and problems yourself… On the plus side, I now have enough t-shirts to last me for life.
- Sustrans talks – I used to charge Sustrans a charity day rate then do as many talks for them as they could fit in. The record: visiting eight schools in a day! It was exhausting but also fun and worthwhile.
- Weddings – I enjoyed photographing a few weddings. But this is indeed proof that I have an unerring and foolish tendency to spread myself too thin rather than concentrating on doing one thing well.

YOU CAN ONLY SAVE ONE: YOUR ABILITY TO RIDE A BIKE OR YOUR SHED WITH ALL ITS CONTENTS.

I have never found any better way to have an adventure than by climbing onto a bicycle and pushing off. The stuff in my shed is only stuff. I carry that lightly and would swap it in an instant for the freedom and adventure of time on a bike.

How much do you earn and does your income vary much?

I am relieved to say that my income does not bounce up and down like an Andean skyline. It pretty much increased steadily each year as my skills and experience grew, until peaking recently.

It took years for me to relax and trust that I was heading in the right direction. Speaking work is very seasonal, so there are often gaps in the year when my diary is empty and everyone seems to have lost interest. My new income was much more haphazard, seasonal and unpredictable than a teacher's. If you are accustomed to a reliable monthly paycheque, this feels unnerving. Thankfully, over time, I can now safely assume that enough work will come my way over the year to even out without having to worry too much about it.

Even so, much of my work is sprinkled with randomness. You don't know when the next speaking request / brand campaign / commissioned article will land in your inbox. Because of the nature of not knowing where my next chunk of income will come from, it is necessary to plan and save on a yearly scale, not a monthly one. Some months I earn nothing at all beyond my passive income! On top of that are the times when I go away on adventures: not only am I spending money, I also miss out on the earning opportunities which come along in that time period. Sod's law particularly enjoys filling my inbox with lucrative offers coinciding with the dates when I am due to be up a hill in my tent.

For that reason, the annual stipends I receive for being a brand ambassador are reassuring, as are the royalty cheques for my books. The sums from each book are not large, but the more books I write, the more substantial a stream those passive income dribbles become.

Passive income is money that you earn without any sustained effort, the very opposite of earning an hourly rate. I like to think of it as making money while you sleep. When I go to bed at night, I snuggle under my duvet knowing that I will have sold a few books by the time I wake up. In an ideal world, I'll get my sales figures up to the point where I can stay under the duvet all day too. Increasing passive income is my long-term financial goal, though I intend to spend those free days in the mountains rather than in bed.

My trickle of passive income should remain pretty steady as long as anyone is still interested in reading my books. By contrast, my brand ambassador work feels more fleeting. Many brands change their marketing teams and ideas more often than I change my pants. Just because I'm interesting and 'on message' for them this year does not mean that will be the case next year. I always consider a brand asking me to stay with them for another year to be a bonus rather than a given. (This, by the way, raises another pressure I feel a lot: the need to keep being visible and relevant so that I remain a marketable 'product'. Much of that last sentence makes me uncomfortable.)

When I cycled around the world, I lived off my savings and enjoyed years of life, adventure and 'content creation' for less than a fiver a day. Once I returned home and began earning again, 90% of my income stemmed from speaking at schools. The remainder came from book sales plus a sprinkling of the additional revenue streams mentioned in the last chapter. Books and talks are an exciting way to pay for a life, and I was comfortable living frugally. My years on the road had taught me to keep the purse strings tight. You can either earn a lot of money or not spend much money – both options work.

To measure whether becoming a Working Adventurer was viable, sustainable and responsible, I set myself the challenge of matching my first year teaching salary in the next year. I just about managed that through giving a lot of talks in schools. I continued to use the teachers' pay scale as my target benchmark for several years to reassure myself that the work I was doing counted as a 'proper job' and that I was on the right trajectory. My memory is hopeless, but I think it probably took about three years before I relaxed about whether the next cheque would ever arrive and about five years before the curve of my income progression began to rise above that of a teacher.

Today, I can focus on getting on with stuff that I enjoy, feels meaningful, and also pays the bills. The score pretty much takes care of itself if I do those things well. That has been a weight off my shoulders.

I don't have any dazzling insights about how to earn more money. I haven't dedicated much brainpower to the puzzle. But I have learned that once you have enough cash, chasing more does not lead to more happiness. The biggest luxury that money provides is not having to worry about money. I am definitely happy to leave behind the years of hustling, chasing and worrying.

My income increased steadily for the first decade, but the percentage splits remained relatively consistent, with 90% coming from speaking work and 10% from books. Over the long term, the percentages have changed as well as the totals. I now earn about 40% from speaking, 40% from brands and 20% from books and podcasts.

My dream for the third decade of my career is to sell many more books (by writing more books rather than suddenly becoming a genius or a celebrity) and be able to live off the royalties alone. Perhaps then I will finally shrug off the imposter syndrome which prevents me from describing myself as a 'writer'. Who knows, in ten years I might write be able to write a book called Ask An Author…

From initial annual earnings of around £30,000 in my first couple of years of self-employment (which I was delighted with), I increased my income more than six-fold. In recent years, I've slowed down my work significantly to become a stay-at-home dad. For environmental reasons, I now routinely decline well-paying speaking events and brand campaigns that require flying. Yet despite these significant restrictions, I still earn a high five-figure sum which is a ridiculously jammy amount for doing work that I love.

WHAT HAS BEEN YOUR FAVOURITE SMALL PURCHASE RECENTLY?
It cost me nothing, but rigging up a pull-up bar behind my shed has had a great impact. Every time I pop out for a pee (pretty often when you spend all day in a shed drinking tea), I blast out a bunch of pull-ups.

How much money does a book like
Microadventures make?

The truthful answer is that I don't know how much money my
Microadventures book makes. Even publishers don't know sales figures
as precisely or as up to date as you might assume. There are issues such
as unsold stock in warehouses, collating reports from all the different
stores, and the publishing industry's general reluctance to acknowledge
that we are in the 21st Century and that the internet is here to stay.

It is not as easy as you'd imagine calculating how many books you
have sold, plus I am hopeless at reading royalty statements or paying
much attention to money. Lest that sounds evasive, I received an
advance of £16,000 for the book. That means I received £4000 on
signing the contract, £4000 on submitting the manuscript, £4000 on
publication and £4000 at some other point which I can't remember.

If that sounds like a lot of money (and I splashed out on building
my writing shed, so I did feel pretty fancy), remember that the book
took a year to write and involved travelling thousands of miles at my
own expense, buying lots of camping and photography equipment and
so forth. Be aware also that an advance is no more than a loan against
future sales. I would not earn another penny from the book until I had
earned out my advance from sales. Most books never manage to earn
out their advance. I don't know how many copies it sold in the first
few years (I asked my publisher for numbers but didn't hear back),
but I began earning royalties reasonably swiftly.

From now on, for as long as *Microadventures* remains in print, I'll
receive 10% of sales (minus the 15% cut my agent gets for negotiating
the deal. The longer a book remains in print, the more massive the
agent's slice feels.)

[A quick aside here. I think these figures are broadly standard. Be
very aware when signing contracts that agents and publishers know
far more about contracts than you do. They are better at negotiating
than you are, and they are trying to earn their living. I've been stung
by a publisher for tiny percentages of a book for the dumb reason
that I was excited to get published, didn't care about money and
thought contracts were too dull to read. I still stand by those points,
but they don't merit getting ripped off. It was very naive of me. I

have also been stung by an agent's commission which riled me for years as being unfairly high. It was, of course, too late to change once I had signed on the dotted line. Don't be like me: seek help from savvy souls before signing contracts.]

I know less than I should about the sales figures for my books, chiefly because royalty statements are incomprehensible to me. I can tell you these snippets after hearing back from one of my publishers. *Moods of Future Joys* has apparently sold 26,000 copies (plus 4,000 self-published copies), although I'm not sure I believe this number. It feels much too low to me. I have spent 14 years flogging it at the back of village halls and on my website and would be surprised if I hadn't sold that many by myself.

On the other hand, the publisher never succeeded in getting the book stocked in any significant quantity in bookshops, so that number may be correct. I did terribly on the contract for that book and only earn 5% of the cover price, except for those I sell on my website, which earn 50%. (Typing this, a wee shudder in the back of my brain suddenly thinks my cut might be as low as 2.5%. I can't bear to dig out the contract to check!) *The Boy Who Biked the World* has sold about 60,000 copies in seven years. Ditto on the contract. I didn't receive an advance for either of those books.

The Doorstep Mile has sold about 4,500 copies so far in its first 15 months. Fortunately, because I self-published this book, it earns a 60% royalty after printing costs, so it has already made me more money than some of my earlier books.

Sales of *Microadventures* are inevitably declining over time, though slowly. They get a boost every summer, and every time I write a new book. (A strong reason for publishing new books is to increase sales of your old books.) If I deciphered my latest royalty statement correctly, I still earn about £8000 a year from *Microadventures*, seven years after publishing it. Potentially I will make something from the book every year for the rest of my life, plus 70 years after my death, so long as it remains in print.

The longer a book stays relevant, the greater the overall earning from the book will be. Books are very much a long tail, slow-burn form of passive income.

I HAVE A NEWBORN. WHAT SIMPLE STORYBOOKS COULD YOU RECOMMEND THAT ARE ABOUT ADVENTURES?

The Snail and the Whale. Also, *A Squash and a Squeeze* has genuinely taught me a lot about life. I quote it surprisingly often.

Who does your tax return and do you have a pension?

I used to do my own tax returns with the assistance of my accountant girlfriend, who found my disorganisation and disinterest very annoying. It was painful and tedious for all parties. Now I pay an accountant to do everything. She tolerates my disorganisation and apathy in exchange for a bill. It is money well-spent.

Every three months, I hand over a big envelope stuffed with receipts and bank statements. I do what my accountant tells me to do and pay what she tells me to pay. I do all this without an iota of understanding. I have no interest in manipulating my tax payments. I earn a comfortable living, did very well in life's lottery (genes, education, family, nationality, etc.), and the least I can do is pay my fair share of taxes to help those who have not been as fortunate.

I have been in the habit of saving money ever since I was a lad on a mission to save up £100 for all the NatWest porcelain piggy banks. I'm happy to live within my means, and saving anything left over comes naturally to me. For years, I simply transferred all my extra money to my wife's bank account, and she chipped away at our mortgage (I think and hope!)

Eventually, I got my act together and started a pension. It only came about because I did a talk for a financial planning company and everyone in the room nagged me to get on with it. So now a very nice man comes to speak to me about once a year. I scrabble around, trying to find him the figures and answers he needs while we have a cup of tea and a biscuit. Eventually, he says, 'I can see that you are glazing over. Don't worry, we're almost done.' And I feel reassured that my future is a little more organised than it was an hour ago.

Here is some very boring but very useful advice to anyone beginning life as a Working Adventurer. Each tip has been learned the hard, painful, boring way:

- Start a separate business bank account.
- Hire an accountant (unless you're a numbers geek).

- Start saving for your future. You're entering, with no safety net, a high-risk career that doesn't favour the old or infirm.
- Not an immediate issue, but an important one: get VAT-registered in good time. I didn't realise that I had reached the threshold for adding VAT to my invoices for a whole year. This led to a very painful saga of having to phone up all my clients and say, 'I don't know if you remember me, but please can I have 20% more money for that work I did ages ago?'

WHAT'S THE WORST WORK DECISION YOU'VE EVER MADE?

Nobody has ever asked me this before, and I'm a bit stumped. I am fortunate never to have had a major disaster. I regret not going big on podcasts when I first dabbled with them way back in 2006 or 2007. Not scrutinising my first publishing contracts before signing them. Ordering 5000 'mappazines' about my India walk. I am tempted to include investing five years of my life in a South Pole expedition that I never got to go on, but that is a regret based on hindsight. I didn't think it was a bad decision at the time, and it almost worked out perfectly.

Does it feel delicious or dirty to earn money from adventure?

There are ups and downs to being paid for what you love doing. I occasionally worry that I am grubbying my love of being in the hills by using those experiences to pay my bills. It also sometimes prompts a bit of online trolling. Earning your living from what is normally a hobby (and a hobby whose values lie far from capitalism) is not always straightforward. It is worth reading the blog post from Tim Moss about why he 'quit being an adventurer to become an accountant'.

Am I destined for decades of telling the same old stories to ever-dwindling audiences in village halls up and down the land? I hope not. At times, I fear so. The solution is that the ways I earn money must evolve as my approaches to adventure evolve, as my career progresses and as I get older.

The role of money in my life has changed a lot since 2002 when I got paid by The Guardian to write my first article. Initially, I worked hard to earn money because I needed to keep afloat and because of the memory of the years when I was skint. Over time my attitude to money changed. Its importance in my work has become more of a measure of my worth.

Because I don't have an annual appraisal or a clear promotion structure, it can be difficult to gauge how well I am doing. My income, therefore, offers an insight into my progress. Most of my satisfaction at being well-paid for something comes from a sense that somebody values my work. There are other measures of success too, less tangible but more meaningful. For example, receiving an email from someone whose life has changed for the better after reading one of my books gives me a warm, fuzzy glow that a bank statement cannot match.

I do not maximise my income well at all (passive income stuff / investing / online courses / hunting for higher-paid talks / writing books based on likely sales levels: stuff like that). I have never been motivated by money, or at least not by the things that money can buy. On the occasions when I have put cash first in thinking about work, I have frequently despised myself. Examples include embarrassing media appearances, naff PR photoshoots or endorsing a product that I don't honestly rate. On the other hand, when I have done something that seems wilfully anti-cash, I often seem to generate more money. I presume this is because it becomes a project that is original, energetic, enthusiastic and authentic.

Over the years, I have earned more (and worked more) than I predicted I would, in no small part to prove to myself that I could make this happen. Nobody was bankrolling me. I am a relaxed fellow and pretty hard to offend. However, there is one occasional misassumption about an adventuring career that riles me. Here it is in the list of questions I received for this book:

> 'Isn't your wife rich? Would you be able to be a 'full time adventurer' if you actually had to pay the bills? The whole adventure scene is un-realistic. It's only rich kids who can afford to do it 'full time'... It's not a real job or something that will pay a continuous wage.'

Yes, my wonderful wife does have a proper job, with grown-up stuff like dress-down Fridays. Yet this has actually resulted in me working far harder than I ever intended to when I set out on this path.

I would feel guilty if I just lazed around all morning (which I have never done even once.) If the sun shines, I go for a run and appreciate that flexibility. But I work so much more consistently than I imagined an adventurer would. Part of this comes from feeling a responsibility to prove I am pulling my weight.

I am more fortunate than most, certainly: I'm a middle-class guy who emerged from university (pre-tuition fees) with not only the benefit of a degree, but also some savings to spend on cycling around the world rather than a mountain of debt. More intangible than the money and the qualifications is the privilege of aspiration. I was brought up hearing that it is a good thing to 'follow your dreams'. I have met and read about many examples of people who have done just that. So it feels normal to me. I have been given permission to dream big and attempt difficult challenges. All of these factors boosted my chances. Yet I don't accept the assumption that I'm a 'rich kid', or sponging off my wife or that it is not a 'real job which pays a continuous wage'.

Being a Working Adventurer entails buying my freedom, independence and creativity at the possible expense of income levels, future security and the self-employed curses of tax returns and invoicing. But if it's a choice between getting rich versus living the life of my choice, then there's no contest for me. Nonetheless, I have ended up earning a comfortable living mostly from what an outsider might perceive to be drinking coffee in a shed or riding a bike and telling an audience about it.

I've often thought that if I became a millionaire, not much would change in my lifestyle, except that I would buy food from delis more often. Jack Johnson sang, 'We've got everything we need right here, and everything we need is enough.' It is a great privilege not to struggle beneath financial worries.

WHAT MAKES AN 'AUTHENTIC' ADVENTURER? CAN YOU SPOT THEM?

They are outdoors doing interesting things, following their own star, not doing Q&As on Instagram.

How do you decide what you will or won't do for money?

There is a paradox in being a Working Adventurer. The challenge is to find a balance between committing to being an 'adventurer' as though it is a serious job with purpose and meaning, whilst also remaining cavalier, carefree and creative.

I would not encourage someone to become a Working Adventurer unless they love the long, lonely, indoor hours of creativity, the organisational challenge of putting out regular content and getting complex projects off the ground, all whilst maintaining the motivation to keep slogging away for years.

When I started out, there was no dilemma about whether or not to accept work opportunities: I needed the money, plus there were very few suitors knocking on my door. So I would have taken anything.

Over time, I got offered more work and also more money for that work. A nice payday can be hard to decline, but I try to remind myself not to be greedy. I always ask myself if this event was taking place tomorrow would I be excited to get out of bed for it or not? If I do not enjoy doing the work, I turn it down. This was one of the main reasons I cut right back on giving interviews or being a guest on podcasts: I don't look forward to doing them.

Deciding whether or not to accept a speaking event boils down to if I am available and whether the fee is high enough to feel worthwhile or the event sounds enjoyable. I'm pickier about the articles I write because they take up writing time, the fees are low, and I don't enjoy doing them. I prefer to save my time and limited brain cells for book writing. I take on articles if the pay is tolerable and the audience reach is significant and relevant or for the pleasant ego boost of writing for a publication I admire.

Making a short film for a company depends upon the nature of the brand, the idea they are hoping to convey, the time commitment, the fee, the location and how much freedom I am given in tackling the brief.

When I remember to do so, I sometimes use affiliate links if I am recommending a book or piece of kit. But I don't take up the regular offers I receive to promote a mishmash of products in return for a commission. It feels a bit tacky and off-message. I don't want to be a salesman. When I try to sell stuff, as I must from time to time, I want it to be worthwhile and relevant, such as my books that I want to reach the biggest possible audience.

By and large, my audience does not want me to be flogging them stuff. They want to read interesting, authentic stories, not paid promotions with staged photos. Regardless of the brand, they tolerate as little marketing as possible. (This is another reason why appropriate, long-term partnerships are far better than single flash campaigns.)

So far, so simple. The dilemmas of what work to accept really arise once I enter the murkier waters of endorsing products, promoting brands and generally being an 'influencer'. That I never do these things for free shows that I classify all this as work, albeit often rewarding work. The best of these situations are when I genuinely like a brand, believe in what they do and would happily pay for the products myself if I was not being paid to use them.

Examples of the strange kaleidoscope of items I have advertised include tents, raincoats and bicycles, as you might expect, but also whisky and banks, jeans and jet skis, luxury watches and white wine, shampoo and shiny trainers, 4x4s and frothy coffee machines. This certainly is not a path I ever imagined treading.

Several years ago, I went on a mission to search for five complementary brands and persuade each to pay me an annual ambassador fee. I pictured an outdoor brand, which seemed obvious. I also hoped to attract car, watch, bicycle, phone and camera companies. My thinking was that these partnerships would free up the time spent chasing articles or talks so that I could concentrate fully on what I love: being out on adventures and telling the stories well, using these products in an organic, authentic way as I did so. I did not succeed at the idea, but the ambassador roles it led to have been a pleasure to be involved with. I'm grateful for the opportunities that resulted from companies such as Mountain Equipment, Haglöfs, The North Face, ViewRanger and Alpkit taking a punt on me.

As with everyone, there are ethical questions over how I choose to earn my money. Is it appropriate to showcase a lifestyle of jetting round the world on adventures, encouraging others to do the same and pollute more? No, not particularly. The same goes for encouraging unnecessary consumption. I should work only with brands that put people and the planet before profit. I should practice what I preach and be mindful of the impact of my actions. After all, the world really does not need more 'stuff'.

Saying 'no' to requests often entails a hefty financial hit, plus missing out on a brilliant trip to film the campaign. So be it. Advertising frivolous stuff is even more damaging than simply buying it myself due to the inherent amplification of advertising.

I must consider my principles before the fee. If I advertise this, will it harm the reputation and goodwill that has taken years to build? Besides, if I feel a bit icky about a proposal, I can be sure that some of my audience will feel the same way and won't be quiet in letting me know if I go ahead with it.

The sectors that I am willing to advertise decrease all the time. I would no longer endorse the diesel-guzzling cars, jet skis, airlines or polluting coffee pods that I have done in the past. I need to be able to look at myself in the mirror in the morning, and that is not a bad deciding factor for all the decisions I make in life. I like money, success, work and applause as much as the next person, but not at the cost of integrity or balance. Adventure meets *Doughnut Economics*: enough is enough.

Without a doubt, there have been times when I've swallowed my pride, sucked up the imagined sniggers of my peers and done an ad for something that doesn't really fit who I am. Simply put, if you have ever rolled your eyes at a brand campaign I have done, then I have decided that the paycheque was worth that response. It feels a bit grubby to write that. Having said that, it made me chuckle to get surprised messages from all the distant corners of my life when I popped up on a cider advert on TV and in cinemas.

I feel a responsibility to give a little back to the wild places that have helped me pay my bills for so long. Companies can choose to become a certified B-Corp or sign up for '1% for the Planet' and give back a small slice of their sales to the environment. With my phobia of paperwork, I have opted instead to simply donate 1% of my pre-tax income (or £1000, whichever is larger each year) to a worthwhile environmental cause. I then make an effort to endorse the work of that charity online, as amplification of positive messages for a social media audience is perhaps the most useful thing I can do, and much better than encouraging them to buy random stuff.

WHAT IS THE MOST UNCOMFORTABLE SITUATION YOU HAVE FOUND YOURSELF IN?

I once woke up in a weather station in Siberia to discover that the nightshift weatherman was now snuggled up naked next to me. In fairness to him, I was in his bed, and he needed somewhere to sleep. This is a story too long for here and better told in the pub...

Does the need to earn money make you a better adventurer?

Until pondering this question, I probably had an inner hunch that adventuring for money slightly tarnishes the experience. I certainly do not like thinking that someone might wrinkle their at something I have done and sniff, 'He's only done that for the money'.

But on reflection, I appreciate that needing to earn money from adventuring has spurred me to be more productive, focused, creative, thoughtful and imaginative.

For example, making money was *not* a factor in any of these:

- Every trip I have ever done.
- My early years of giving school talks.
- Speaking events that are intriguing, for charity or an honour.
- A fair amount of my blogging.
- A few of my books, including *Moods of Future Joys*, the first instalment of *The Boy Who Biked the World* and *My Midsummer Morning*.
- My film, Into the Empty Quarter.
- The first two seasons of my Living Adventurously podcast.

Earning money *was* a factor in these activities:

- My other books, most notably my foray into the world of producing notebooks. I hope they are genuinely useful, but they are also an unashamed effort to sell blank paper like Wernham Hogg!
- My other podcasts (There Are Other Rivers and The Doorstep Mile). I had already recorded them as audiobooks and it was easy to convert them into another format.
- The My Midsummer Morning film was a disaster in terms of money as I spent quite a lot to get it made and barely anyone has watched it on YouTube.
- Adverts for brands.
- The vast numbers of blog posts I spent years writing to build content / SEO / expertise.
- Most corporate talks. They are usually enjoyable, but they are also a job.

- My newsletters.
- Social media.

Whilst it has always been important to keep myself in check by asking, 'Would I do this if nobody found out about it?', I do feel that the need to earn money has made me a better Working Adventurer. Through it I have explored different ideas, different places, different types of journey and different ways of communicating. All that has raised adventure above being a mere hobby and the pleasure of riding my bike and going camping. It has motivated me to grow communities, evangelise about participating in adventures, and also to think, read, and write more deeply about subjects I hope other people may find helpful.

WHAT SHOULD I DO ABOUT BEING TOO COMFORTABLE WITH THE WAY THINGS ARE, EVEN THOUGH I KNOW I'M NOT HAPPY?

What would the 80-year-old version of yourself advise you to do? And when would they recommend you begin it?

How do you get companies to support your adventures?

Some expeditions are prohibitively expensive. The only realistic option for most of us who want to cross an ocean or trek to the poles is to persuade a company to finance the trip in return for publicity, motivating their staff or product testing.

Whilst finding a sponsor for an adventure sounds like heaven, there are several caveats worth bearing in mind before getting too excited. First, you will relinquish some of the freedom that all good adventures have. Second, you may lose some control of your plans and story-telling voice. Third, the pursuit of sponsors may lead to delays in beginning your journey. Above all, it is tough to persuade a company to pay for your adventure of a lifetime. The odds are stacked against you.

So do you really need sponsors? Can you come up with a more affordable and equally captivating idea? Must you have the most up-to-date equipment? Buying cheap stuff on eBay might be easier than being rejected by a hundred companies. Rather than all the stress, slog, disappointment and loss of self-respect that goes into chasing sponsors, could you just stay in your job for a bit longer and save up your own money? Put £20 aside every week over a year of planning, and by the time you are organised, fit, and free of commitments, you will have saved enough to cycle thousands of miles and have a grand adventure. If you are willing to travel more frugally, your money will take you further. Halve your daily expenditure and double the duration of your expedition.

Having failed to find a financial sponsor myself, I didn't have enough money to cycle around the world when I set off, but I was reluctant to delay. So I just slept wild in my tent, lived off banana sandwiches and eked out my money to make it last.

As I wrote on my blog after that journey, reflecting on the challenges of sponsorship:

"'Do you really think we just got off the banana boat?" said the latest letter.

"Riding a BICYCLE round the WORLD?! If you want a bike why not get a job like everybody else. Nobody is going to fall for such a ridiculous suggestion."
My search for sponsors to support my idea of cycling round the planet was not going well.'

All in all, finding sponsors is not easy.

But let's assume that my bucket of well-meaning cold water has not extinguished your enthusiasm. What are the next steps to take? Most of the same principles apply whether you are after expedition funding or a partnership ambassador role.

You will have to sell yourself: loads of folk are planning fascinating journeys and asking for similar things. No company is going to come knocking on your door begging to give you money and shiny equipment. So what can you offer in return for their support?

Come up with a plan that gets you very excited. So excited that you want to start right this minute. Now go for a long run with your pessimist's hat on. What's wrong with your plan? What are the risks, pitfalls and hurdles?

All good adventure plans are simple. Can you explain it in just a few sentences? It is always evident in my talks that the audience is more interested in simple A to B projects than convoluted ventures. Occam's Razor is usually right.

So much has already been done that it is very difficult to persuade a sponsor that your plans are sufficiently different to stand out. Sponsors won't care if you plan to walk one thousand miles on broken glass in your underpants if a celebrity has already done that for two minutes on TV. It's all the same to most people. Nobody cares about the small details of your adventure in the way that you do.

You need to be original without selling out or becoming a silly gimmick. (Integrity is worth more than sponsorship.) You need to big up the thrills for your audience and simultaneously downplay the risks. Don't lie about anything, but think creatively about how you can tell your story. Don't offer more than you will be able to deliver: promise low, deliver high. You are trying to persuade somebody to pay you to go away and do the most exciting thing you have ever done. Why should they? What will you provide in return for their support? Why are you and your adventure different to all the others?

What is your clear and unique selling point? This question is vital, and you need to be able to answer it in a single sentence, a single page and, eventually, in a long conversation with a prospective sponsor. Why should they care?

Local companies are likely to be satisfied with some press coverage of your adventure, and local newspapers are always desperate for stories. So this is probably your easiest opening gambit.

Niche product suppliers will be interested in you testing their gear to destruction and writing on your blog for others with similar interests. Publicity is like oxygen for most sponsors: get up on the rooftops (Page 1 of Google) and start hollerin'.

Make your requests personal and specific. What, exactly, do you need – and why? Build your reputation up from the bottom. Getting sponsored kit is relatively achievable and realistic. Getting cash is much, much harder. I failed to find anyone to support my 46,000-mile ride around the planet with money or even a bicycle. All I managed to source were water bottles, shoes, trousers, two pairs of socks and a free penknife. I loved that penknife.

Start your quest for sponsorship through your network of family, neighbours, colleagues, classmates, friends and friends of friends. It's not what you know; it's who you know. Sad, but true. Don't get a chip on your shoulder if you don't know anyone suitable; most people have no valuable connections or contacts when they begin. Do interesting stuff, make yourself more interesting, think laterally, search more widely. Get out there and meet people. Your network is your net worth, remember, and by far your best opportunity to get in touch with the person who holds the purse strings in the company you're targetting.

When drawing up a list of businesses to contact, think laterally. How many sponsorship requests for climbing expeditions must The North Face receive? The young Bear Grylls was on the right lines when he dropped off his proposal for an Everest climb at a random company called Davis Langdon and Everest, purely because of the company's name. They bit. He summited.

Whilst a personal connection is best, a specific email to the right person (rather than the generic info@brand.com address) is your second best option and the approach you'll need to go for most of the time. Save yourself a lot of time: cold calling and spam emailing random companies does not work.

Social media is not a bad third option for getting a brand to notice you and answer your enquiry. Look for where they connect with their audience online, study how they interact and what they respond to, then send them a carefully worded message.

However you get in touch with someone, do your best to write correctly. Write individual emails rather than launching bulk email grenades. Put your apostrophe's in the right places. Spell names correctly. We're not all poets, but we've all got spell-checkers. Like so much of this, it's not about spelling; it's about effort and dedication and attitude.

Outline who you are, what you are doing, and why the company would benefit from partnering with you. You need to be able to get someone excited about your trip very quickly. This person has many emails to deal with, and they probably receive a fair few just like yours. Master your elevator pitch, how you'd describe your adventure to Elon Musk if you found yourself in a lift with him.

Save the eye-watering details of how much loot you are after for a second conversation. Your main aim with your first contact should be to secure a second conversation, nothing more. Don't expect an immediate reply from busy people, but do follow up if you have not had a response in a couple of weeks. Pester away, but don't be a pest.

When you finally secure a face to face meeting, you can then play the trump card of turning up with a big map. It never fails to impress and makes your appointment stand out from their routine daily business. Bring the excitement of your adventure into the office. I once arrived at my publisher's labouring beneath a vast rucksack stuffed with all my camping gear and a packraft as I was due to catch a train to Scotland later that day. Years later, the publisher still chuckles about that and tells the tale in every meeting we have.

As with every meeting in life, do not be late. I have had a couple of important meetings where I was so determined to be punctual that I actually did a test run of the trains and underground the week before, just to make sure! You might prefer to settle for arriving a couple of hours early, scoping out the venue, then going to a café (not a pub) to practice your pitch and soothe your nerves.

I wish you well in the quest for funding support. It is an aspect of my working life that I dislike and am not good at. I hope you have more success than me. However, do continue to remind yourself of why you began all this in the first place. Was it to faff with website re-design, schmooze with potential sponsors and edit spreadsheets? Or was it to get out there, feel alive and do something to make you proud?

If all else fails, get a job and buy the stuff you need second hand. If you can't afford your idea, do something cheaper. Save up, sell everything you don't need (most stuff), get on your bike and pedal away into the sunset. Don't allow searching for sponsors to be an excuse for delay or procrastination.

WHAT HAVE YOU IDENTIFIED AS THE BIGGEST CHALLENGES IN PROMOTING AN ADVENTUROUS LIFESTYLE?

When trying to evangelise about why someone should try their first microadventure, I focus on promoting the idea that doing a little is better than nothing and that little spare time does not mean zero spare time. I try to emphasise all the good aspects of what might happen rather than getting hung up on one over-hyped worry (monsters, the cold, sheep, etc.). These seem to address the major objections people raise to the idea of an adventurous lifestyle.

What advice would you give a 45-year-old single guy with a very good job paying over 100,000 euros a year? Should he carry on with his secure job or stop?

It is hard to answer this question when I only have one metric for measuring it. Yes, you earn 100,000 euros. But are you happy? Are you making the world a better place or a worse place? It's similar to countries measuring success by GDP whilst ignoring life expectancy, happiness, equality or sustainability. Try measuring yourself against the 'Happy Planet Index' or the 'Happiness Index' calculated in Bhutan and New Zealand and see if those help you answer your question.

If you hate the job, quit today. You've almost reached life expectancy in Sierra Leone. Don't waste any more of your time. The website www.DeathClock.com will show you, starkly, how finite life is and how stupid and sad it is to waste it if you have other options. Read the brilliant but alarming 'Tail End' post on the Wait But Why blog. It is a magnificent wake-up call.

If you don't mind your job, ask yourself how much money you *need* each year. Ask how much money you *want* each year. Think about the implications of the difference between those figures, not only in terms of the shiny toys you'd like to buy, but also the hours of your life you need to exchange to buy them.

Calculate the money you need to mitigate against sickness and disaster. Read *The 100-Year Life* and plan for a viable pension. Do not plan to become the richest man in the graveyard.

Now that you are clearer about your financial requirements, think about cutting back your work. Would a four-day week give you enough time to chase your dreams? How about asking for a month of unpaid leave each year?

What are you itching to do whilst stuck in that well-paid job of yours? What do you love doing? Is there a job that would pay you to do some of those things? Might this career be an avenue that interests you? For example, you could be a full-time nurse but also explore other countries by working for the international humanitarian organisation Médecins Sans Frontières. You could be a piano tuner but earn your living by cycling around the world tuning pianos along the way (an actual dream of a friend of mine).

I think the fact that you have asked this question suggests that you know, deep down, whether you should continue with your well-paid, secure job or do something different. Don't make a decision simply by not making a decision.

DO YOU THINK IT'S EVER TOO LATE TO START ADVENTURING, GIVEN GENERAL GOOD HEALTH BUT INEVITABLY BEING LESS AGILE THAN WHEN YOUNG?

No, I do not think it is ever too late to begin. There are many pros and cons around what age is best for adventuring. Youth offers energy and idealism. With age comes wisdom, a maturity of observation, improved communication skills and a buffer of cash. I am confident that the best time to begin adventuring was many years ago. The second best time is now.

My newsletters have a high number of retired readers, many of whom are living really adventurous lives. If you would like to read about some inspiring, older adventurers, check out the books of Rosie Swale Pope, Audrey Sutherland, Dervla Murphy and Aleksander Doba.

Would you rather have a fulfilling, high-paying but extremely demanding job with little free time, or a job that is not as fulfilling, 9-5, but still well-paid and with more free time for travelling? I'm a 19-year-old trying to make the right decision for my future.

I think your conundrum boils down to the difference between a 'vocation' and a 'job'. I remember reading once that part of the reason a medical degree begins with swathes of seemingly irrelevant science and statistics modules is to weed out those who don't want it badly enough. I doubt this is technically true, but there is some sense to it. I once turned up for an Army selection course where the first thing they made us do was run up and down the car park until we puked. Those who didn't want it enough were in and out of the door in less than an hour. I remember one guy walking out of the barbed wire gates before we had even finished running! Is there a job that you would run till you puked to secure? It is likely to be something that prioritises purpose, which feels like the right thing to do through good times and bad.

When I was 19, I had no idea what career I wanted to do, so don't feel pressured to decide. I'd urge you to try to keep your options open and make an effort not only to find what you enjoy but also to eliminate what you *don't* want to do for the next 50 years. Don't worry about getting rich or leaping up the career ladder yet. Instead, taste the possibilities of the universe. Get out and explore. Look for opportunities. Be wary of so-called 'inherited wisdom' or preconceptions of what people like you are 'supposed' to do with your lives. Society places a considerable amount of subconscious expectations on all of us.

Remember that most people who are in a position to offer you balanced and reasonable advice (me included) made their big life decisions in a very different world to yours: pre-COVID, Bitcoin, Zoom or Instagram, before the financial crash, Brexit, climate panic and any number of other massive factors that will influence your working life and goals. We might have helpful perspectives, but we also don't see the world in the same way that you do.

Career advice has always been a hopeless art. It was terrible back 'in my day'. (My school suggested I should become either an actuary, a librarian or a pharmacist.) It is even more so today when nearly all the 'grown ups', whose advice you might respect, have no idea about careers that did not even exist a decade ago. Instead, find an internet niche that excites you and listen to how those experts reflect about their lives. (Remember also that behind the slick blog, the enviable social media profile, and the seemingly idyllic life is a whole iceberg of hard work, uncertainty and all those who didn't make it to the top.)

When the time comes for you to choose a job, if you still have not found anything that thrills you and fills you with purpose, then go for the job that gives you the maximum cash in exchange for the fewest possible hours of your life. I hope, however, that you can find something that not only pays the bills but also feels worthwhile and enjoyable. Good luck.

DO YOU HAVE ANY ADVICE FOR YOUNG PEOPLE ON HOW TO LIVE LIFE AND NOT JUST SURVIVE?

Read a lot. Listen to challenging and educational podcasts. Save as much money as you can. Read *The Hundred Year Life*, *Man's Search for Meaning* and a book on Stoicism. Go to new nearby places. Try different activities. Meet people from a range of backgrounds and cultures. Be in a hurry. Be patient. Fear regrets, not failures. Try to appreciate that you will never have so much spare time again. Pursue projects that interest you, not what everyone else is doing.

TIME

How do you avoid a conflict between your adventures, your work and your family?

My first reaction to this question was 'mind your own business'. But seeing as this is a book based on inviting readers to ask me anything, that wasn't very fair! I prefer to keep my 'work' life and my 'real' life completely separate, just as you might if you were a physiotherapist or a fishmonger. It's a matter of both privacy and relevance.

The matter of spending time away from your family is a personal one. I see some people clucking endlessly around their family, the kids their only focus, and suspect it would benefit not only them but also their whole family if they went away on an adventure occasionally and bloomed a little. It might spark some crazy passion in the children too.

On the other hand, I think of other folk I know and regard the amount of time they spend away from their young family to be excessive.

In other words, this whole subject is similar to travelling on a motorway: anyone driving slower than me is a moron; anyone who overtakes me is a lunatic...

Some, I suspect, ask how I balance adventure with commitments out of envy and general curiosity: they would love to have more free time (as would I). They say things like 'I wouldn't be allowed so much time off'. What is the secret? What are my lifehacks?

Others might ask as an accusation of selfishness, 'How can you go on adventures whilst leaving a partner and children at home?' What efforts do you make to redress the balance?

I don't deny the selfish label entirely, but I hope my answer will soften it a little. I certainly try very hard to make sure it is not the case.

The struggle between family time and adventure time is my single greatest working challenge. It is continuously frustrating, despite how it might appear from my Instagram feed. In basic terms, my scope for adventure has decreased massively with family life. Of course it has: more often than not 'adventure' is linked with 'freedom', 'time', 'solitude' and 'risk'. They are pretty different drivers to an outing to feed the ducks.

I am well aware of the difficulty of fulfilling your commitments whilst also trying to get your personal adventure kicks in what feel to be tiny windows of free time. We are all so busy. It is difficult to pay due attention to all your roles in life: family member, friend, worker and individual.

However, adventure is not only something I enjoy; it is also my job. That puts me in a slightly different position to many others who wish they had more time to go on adventures. For example, whilst my wife was taking time off work for maternity leave, we hired an au pair to help at home, and then I set off to row the Atlantic Ocean. It was terrible timing, but it was a rare and excellent opportunity, an important expedition that would boost my writing and speaking work. Would I have done the trip if nobody ever found out? From a work point of view, definitely not. It was very much an expedition to help with my career. Yet it also happened to be a hell of a personal adventure.

A succinct summary of that experience would be to say that I was wracked with guilt to be leaving my lovely wife with the burden of a baby whilst I went and did something dangerous. My wife, in return, was not thrilled with my latest exotic 'holiday'. That was entirely understandable. The solution was not as simple as me taking a year's paternity leave from my work whilst she returned to the office, for she wanted to be at home. But let's just say that the expensive satellite phone calls back home from mid-Atlantic were terse.

For a few years after becoming a father, I tried to carry on with the adventuring side of my life as though nothing had changed, building towards an epic journey to the South Pole. But in the end, the complications of real life dismantled that dream. It was just not compatible with conventional family life. I pulled out of the South Pole trip and all future huge expeditions. This left me feeling diminished and disappointed, frustrated and unhappy.

In *My Midsummer Morning*, I wrote, 'You cannot go alone into the wilderness for months and also be a stay-at-home dad. You cannot teeter across a crevasse field without feeling somewhat reckless. And when I do manage to get away – to make a short film, for example – I know people frown on it as 'going on holiday' rather than 'going to work'. My life, my work, my hobby: it is all the same thing. It is me. I cannot compartmentalise things in the way many parents do, swapping stuff around, cutting down on hobbies or pausing bits for a decade.'

Nobody asks lorry drivers or consultants how they 'get so much time away from their family' to go and do their job. It is accepted that some positions require long hours at the office or time out on the road. But when your work revolves around going on fabulous trips, questions inevitably get asked about your commitment to domestic responsibilities.

It seemed to me at the time that all the people asking this chapter's question were correct: it was not possible to go away on the journeys that my career, my ambition and my restlessness demanded, whilst also being at home with the children I loved and helping my wife to flourish. Blessed indeed are the parents who can gain all the nourishment and inspiration they need from within the routines and rhythms of normal family life.

If you are considering stepping away from a conventional job to become a Working Adventurer, you need to consider the impact that it will have on your family as well as on yourself. Until you arrive at a point (hopefully) where you are earning what all parties involved deem to be an acceptable income, it can be hard to justify going away a lot. This is particularly true if your other half works in a more traditional environment and thinks in terms of guaranteed salaries, nine to five hours and weekends weeding the flower beds, like most folk.

For example, are you developing the skills you need to earn a comfortable living as a film-maker, or are you 'just spending day and night playing with your little videos'?

Are you investing in the equipment you need to do your work to the high standards you have set yourself, or are you 'buying more camping stuff and camera toys for your hobbies when you haven't even got a job'?

And are you grafting away building up the experience and stories you need to become respected as a well-paid, professional story-teller, or are you 'taking yourself off on another bloody holiday'?

(These examples are works of fiction. Any resemblance to actual events is purely coincidental. Probably.)

OK, enough of the disclaimers: I suspect I'm not getting a lot of sympathy. Here is how I attempt to make everything work, to be present for my children, to pull my weight at home, to ensure my wife has all the time she needs for her work and her life, but also to keep the wheels going as a Working Adventurer.

For various reasons, our family can't go and cycle around the world together, walk across the Outback with a toddler in a buggy or live off grid in a cabin in Alaska. And I do not want to go away from home extended periods on my own and miss out on the marvellous mayhem and hullabaloo of my kids growing up. I want to be right in the middle of it all with them. I have accepted the incompatibility, chosen my priority and tolerated the decrease in adventures (and with that the earning potential potential and so on).

The number of questions I received on this subject showed me that I am not alone in trying to fit in too many incompatible activities. The huddled masses of adventurous souls yearning to breathe free out in the hills is what made *Microadventures* my most helpful book. It was trying to combine my desire for adventure, the need to keep my career alive and the importance of remaining at home for my family that ushered in the era of 'microadventures'. I began trying to seek short, simple, local alternatives to longer journeys, asking myself what opportunities remained for adventure rather than lamenting life's constraints.

My wife has one day off from work a week when she does the school run, and I can dash off for an overnight microadventure. That is how I make many of my short films, for example. I leave home at about 9 pm once the children are in bed and drive north powered by

Radio 4 and fresh fruit. I reach the hills at 3 am, sleep in the car till dawn, then run around all day filming stuff. Then I drive back home through the night powered by Haribo sweets and house music in time to take the kids to school.

I am trying to learn how to combine my 'adventure life' with my 'normal life'. It is not easy. Yet, I am also becoming increasingly convinced that it is better to pursue a lifetime of living a little bit adventurously every day rather than dreaming of an adventure of a lifetime one day.

My 'adventuring' generally takes place between 9 am and 3 pm from Monday to Friday during school term times, if such a thing sounds possible. The rest of the time, I am Dad / family taxi driver / chef / laundry man, all of which is filled with its own adventures and challenges. I don't go away at weekends or do speaking events then so that I can take the kids to their clubs and give my wife plenty of peace and quiet after her busy week of work. I don't work in the school holidays. And the less said about the delights of the year of Coronavirus homeschooling, the better.

I do my best to squeeze in my adventure fixes around the margins of my days and make do with the suburban and semi-rural landscapes of southern England where I live. I swim in rivers for a taste of freedom. I climb a tree at least once a month to keep connected with nature. These small moments also help me be a kinder, calmer, more interesting husband, father and person.

I am fortunate to get to do as much as I do. But my circumstances are also not exceptional, perhaps, beyond my 30 hours of weekly 'work', which pleasingly often involves going for a bike ride and putting it on Facebook. Most of what you see of me on the internet these days comes from trying to practise what I preach: the world of 5-to-9 microadventures or lunchtime escapes.

There are some exceptions to this routine and occasions when I do still go away from longer periods. For example, I busked through Spain for four weeks in 2016 whilst my heroic wife kindly took up the slack of summer holiday childcare. In 2019 she decided to take unpaid leave to spend more time with the children, so I nipped off to cycle around Yorkshire for four weeks and record a podcast. I seized on that opportunity to hit the road before returning for our family holiday together.

The adventures I choose nowadays are based on questions of efficiency. Not just 'will this be a good laugh?' but also 'can I squeeze it into less time away?' It is a consequence of trying to earn a living from what I love. I am highly conscious of how I use every hour. It definitely involves a lot of planning, compromise, rushing and efficiency.

WHAT ARE YOUR VIEWS ON WILD CAMPING, TRESPASS AND ACCESS TO MUCH OF THE COUNTRYSIDE POTENTIALLY BECOMING CRIMINAL OFFENCES?

I think it is ridiculous how much of our countryside is enclosured and out of reach. Criminalise trespassers who wreck places, yes, but not hikers and lovers of wild places.

If you were single and had no kids, what would you do differently?

Hmmm... I've never thought about this question. OK, here are 999 things I've imagined a million times in the years of nappies and sleepless nights.

Like many hypothetical questions, this one requires me to hold two opposing, contradictory, but true ideas in my head at once: knowing that I'd be devastated if I *was* suddenly single and childless, yet also imagining that reality had never existed and therefore feeling free and agile.

Above all else, if I somehow woke up in a different reality, I would marvel at how much time and money I suddenly had. In other words, I have become a boring old man moaning that 'youth is wasted on the young' or advising expectant parents to 'get some sleep'.

I would spend most of my time either away on adventures or working in my shed. I could do that quite happily from dawn till dusk seven days a week. I get excited just imagining how much I would suddenly be able to get done as well as all the adventures I could go on.

I would be driven to use that extra time and treasure it, far more than I ever did back in the days when I took the commodity for granted. I used to assume that time would last forever. Nowadays, I feel as though I will never have enough again. The wisest book I have read on this subject, by the way, is *A Squash and a Squeeze* by Julia Donaldson. And I have read that book a *lot* of times.

The question led me onto a detour of thinking about what I could have done differently in my life and how I could have used my time better. Perhaps such musings are futile at best, harmful at worst. They certainly can't change anything in my past. But it is never too late to start filling your days closer to the brim.

The removal of ties and commitments would free me to dare to be more audacious. Those who are bold enough to make big changes to their direction often report that the consequences were not nearly so binding as they feared beforehand. Often you don't know if the 'mistakes' you make along the way are actually mistakes or just forks in the road. Hindsight might reveal them to be lessons or blessings in disguise.

I would explore more directions and take more risks. Creative risks. Adventurous risks. Financial risks. Don't be cavalier with your money, but do spend it generously on activities that are educational, creative, purposeful, philanthropic or adventurous. You can always make more money, but you cannot always get more freedom. And you can never make more time.

As well as becoming really bold, I would be in even more of a hurry than usual. I have always been in a hurry. It worked very well before becoming a parent but has been something of a nightmare to un-learn in worlds where life runs more smoothly with extended time frames and lower ambitions.

What would a tree do if it magically swapped its roots for legs? I reckon the first thing for Madam Oak would be to have a look around and get a different perspective from the one it has always had. Before you have roots, chase your enthusiasms and your curiosities wherever they lead.

What else would I advise? Don't dream: go out to explore and discover. Go on a journey. Travel while you can with whatever money you can spare. Live cheap and rough and revel in the simplicity and emancipation of that. Go places you have never been. Meet people who look at the world differently. Learn from them. Dive deeply into niches that interest you, whatever they may be. Hone your talents. Follow your curiosity resolutely until it blooms into a passion. Who knows, you might even be able to make it your job one day.

I can also answer this chapter's question with some specific examples. I would spend a year or two living in America, basing myself for a month or so in different towns and blasting around doing microadventures in the astonishing variety of wild places there. Or perhaps I would load up a camper van with bikes and boats and books, then drive around the Deep South, eating in tiny diners, chatting and taking photographs. Or I might just set off on my bike again and keep going. Then I would spend a month in San Francisco and a month in NYC (cycling between the two) to write a 'Microadventures USA' book. I love America; diners, blue highways, and so much empty space...

I could fill page after page with lists of all the global journeys I dream of taking one day. Yet, most of my travels in the past decade have been closer to home, and as I contemplate this hypothetical sudden freedom, I also think about a circumnavigation of Britain. The Munroes. The Scottish islands. All the bothies. There is a completist, trainspotter-type urge within me when I contemplate endless time and no ties.

But the nomadic idea of these adventures doesn't thrill me quite as much as it used to. My impulses have softened with time and plenty of miles on the clock.

For example:

- At 24, I'd have chosen to go on a colossal, cheap, roaming, hard, inquisitive global bicycle journey. I would recommend that to anyone.
- At 34, I was desperate to go on an expedition to the South Pole, make my mark professionally, push my physical limits with something to be proud of, and impress others. Perhaps that is not what I'd encourage a single 34-year-old to do today, but it is what fired me at that age.
- At 44, what appeals to me now is a community, friends who lend me books, talk about events beyond our horizon and go for runs before breakfast. I dream of collaborative creative projects, taking photographs, a local hill to sleep on, a nearby river or ocean to swim in, a busy local café and acres of time to appreciate these things. Every couple of months, I'd saddle up and go on a long, slow journey for a while. Then, every year or two, I'd swap my lovely village for a different landscape and enjoy exploring from the beginning all over again.

Right now, I'd like to live in a village or small town in the hills or on the coast, turn off my computer, delete my emails and social media and live a life filled with friends, outdoor exercise, books to read and time to be creative. That is what I dream of.

What I have found most interesting about pondering this question, and somewhat unsettling, is that what I would choose to do if I was single is entirely compatible to doing with a family.

Food for thought.

WHAT IS YOUR FAVOURITE WAY TO SPEND TIME?

There is so much that I love to do. Watching sport in a pub with friends. Arriving somewhere I have never been before. Sitting in a café in a town where nobody knows my name, with a notepad and a good book. Editing a book I have nearly finished writing. Filming an adventure. Cycling downhill. Running uphill. Watching the sunrise. Swimming in rivers and waterfalls and oceans. Eating spicy food. Opening a cold beer on a warm evening. Buying a map. Waking up outdoors. Cooking on a fire. Laughing round the kitchen table.

How do you get your work done?

I might have been surprised by how many questions I received about my daily routine, except that I am also a sucker for this sort of information. I enjoyed the book *Daily Rituals* and fell into the usual trap of thinking, 'If only I have breakfast at the same time Beethoven did, I'll be much more efficient!' (Bad example: Beethoven was deliciously slovenly and chaotic.) Followed by, 'If only I heed the lessons of *Deep Work* and focus without distraction,' I muse, deep in procrastination, 'all will be well.' And, finally, 'Let me just check Twitter one more time before I get down to work.'

So with the caveats that I am permanently frustrated about how little time I have, how much of it I waste, how inefficiently I work and how I am too much of a control freak to delegate well, here's how I use my time and how I get my work done.

I am very fortunate that my job is my hobby. I love settling down to work. Monday morning is my favourite time of the week. Since I became a Working Adventurer, I have always worked from home. At times, I have worked in the spare bedroom or from the sofa. I worked for a while in an attic that was so hot I had to strip to my boxers, thankfully before the era of Zoom calls. I once set up a desk in a conservatory for a few months, hiding under an umbrella when the sun was too bright to see my computer screen. I've written blog posts whilst eating breakfast and edited book chapters on the loo. I tackle my email inbox whilst on taxi duty, waiting to collect my kids from various clubs. Right now I am scribbling down a few thoughts for this chapter whilst cooking my lunch (mushrooms and tomatoes on toast).

I began yearning for a specific workspace of my own. A place where I could think, 'This is where I work. Today, I will grind out some creativity and get a thousand words written no matter how little I feel like it.' (There's a difference between grinding out reluctant creativity and the sparkling creativity which comes from long runs, visiting new places and drinking coffee with interesting people.) I also wanted a place that would help me separate my work life from the rest of my life.

I would happily work all day, every day. The only trouble with this is that it's hard to stop. I don't dash out of the office on a Friday and forget about everything for the weekend. My work is never finished. There is always more that I could do, always more that I would like to do. It can become a bit of an obsession.

Rather than working in the house, I wanted to go to work and then come home later and relax, as normal people do. This separation felt like a necessary and helpful demarcation for me to make. So I spent the first chunk of my advance for writing *Microadventures* building a shed in the garden, wallpapering the walls with the maps I used during the writing of that book. It has been a brilliant investment. My shed has become my office, my refuge, my commute and a constant source of inspiration and satisfaction.

On a weekday morning, I open up my shed after doing the school run. The heater in my shed is on a timer switch, making it nice and toasty when I arrive. I connect my laptop and switch on the power. The kettle and radio burst into life, already primed to go the night before.

I try to resist the tyranny of the email inbox and instead get to work on what, at the end of the previous day, I had deemed to be my three most important tasks and stuck to my monitor on a Post-It note. I am usually on a roll when I have to stop for the day. So I am kind to my future self by telling the procrastinating 'morning me' what to get on with. It's a writing trick that Hemingway used, 'The best way is always to stop when you are going good and when you know what will happen next. If you do that every day... you will never be stuck.'

The day's three most important tasks vary, but most of the time they include getting 1000 words written. That target is more tangible than 'do a lot of writing' and less open to interpretation and faff than 'do four hours of writing'. I try to blitz it before I get tired or distracted. I don't find writing to be a breeze. It is more like a daily ordeal I wrestle with. Distraction and procrastination are nightmare foes in the age of the internet. It can be a lonely world being a writer with nobody holding you to account. It is easy to drift off course and lose your way, particularly if you don't have the support of an agent, an editor or a publisher.

I usually manage to write for about 45 minutes before I need to divert my brain. That might mean putting the kettle on or going outside to do some pull-ups. Then I do another 45 minutes. I repeat these sprints until I have reached my day's target.

That's pretty much the only advice I have about 'how to write a book'. Don't check your emails. Don't wait for the muse to strike. Write 1000 words at the start of every working day. Ninety days later, you'll have finished the first draft of your book. Crime writer Michael Gilbert, for example, wrote 30 novels exclusively during his train commute to and from work over many years.

Once I have bashed out my ration of words, I treat myself to the little dopamine hits of opening my emails, skimming my RSS feeds (with Feedly) and answering my Twitter @replies. It is usually late morning by now. I have an early, high-speed lunch, then return to my shed for a couple more hours working on projects, editing, planning, admin, or more writing. My alarm goes off at 2.30 pm, and I begin shutting everything down for the day. I stick a Post-it note to my monitor with the three most important tasks I need to tackle tomorrow, top up the kettle for the morning, then set off to do the school run at the end of another day's work.

HOW DO YOU MOTIVATE YOURSELF TO GO ON A RUN?

I often struggle to motivate myself to exercise, mainly because I usually have to do it late at night. I have a rule that I only have to put my trainers on and run to the end of the road. After that, I can come home and eat cake if I'm not in the mood for exercise. However, by the time I get to the end of the road, I always just keep going. The doorstep mile is the hardest one.

How do I have a gap year now that I am 40 with kids and bills?

If you want to have a gap year but have a mesh of commitments, one option is to quit your job, sell all your stuff, pack up the family and hit the road together. A serious question: what is stopping you from doing that, beyond fear, inertia and convention? Do you think you would regret that decision when looking back on your life?

Another option could be to tighten your belt, save up, then take as much time off as your boss and budget will allow. Does that sound more feasible?

These are questions about the concept of a gap year and your mindset rather than specifics and practicalities. They are about society's priorities, assumptions and preconceptions and the way they might have influenced your own more than you realise.

Here is a third possibility: the standard British worker has 112 days off each year. What could you and your family do with all that time if you made a concerted effort to live more adventurously? What places could you explore? What challenges and projects could you tackle? What weekend adventures might await? You could cycle to the ocean, swim in rivers and sleep under the stars in places you have never been before.

If your work is so demanding that you are too busy to be able to countenance a few evenings out on a hilltop, may I be so bold as to suggest that you are exactly the sort of person who would benefit the most from watching a few sunrises and sunsets? As the saying goes, 'You should sit in nature for twenty minutes every day unless you're too busy; then you should sit for an hour.'

If you don't feel able to indulge in a full gap year, perhaps you and your kids could make this your 'gap year of microadventure' together?

SHOULD I GO ON AN ADVENTURE BEFORE OR AFTER UNIVERSITY IF IT'S A TWO-YEAR TRIP THAT I CAN'T FIT INTO A GAP YEAR?

Go on your adventure before university, if possible. It will put you on a much better footing for all aspects of university life. I would always encourage you to travel as early as you can afford to do. Life will only ever get more tangled, complicated and busy. You'll never again have as much spare time or freedom of choice as you do today, or at least not until your knees are knackered and you're sporting a blue rinse at the bingo hall.

What advice would you give parents to encourage their kids to be adventurous rather than fearful about what could go wrong?

First of all, I am reluctant to offer any parenting advice. It insinuates a mastery that I do not feel!

Disclaimer over: I would say lead by example. I see parents in playgrounds urging their kids to try the monkey bars or climb the nets, whilst they remain firmly rooted to a bench glued to their phones. If my children aren't in the mood to climb a tree, I just go ahead and climb it myself. They soon join me.

Kids pick up on all your cues. Are you encouraging them to explore and excited about what will probably go well, or are you fearful of all that might go wrong? Are you leading by example by trying new things yourself, risking failure and embarrassment along the way? This was one reason why I began learning the violin to go and busk through Spain and the main reason I enjoyed doing parent-child taekwondo classes for years. I was rubbish. My hips hurt, and my high kicks were knee-high. Yet I listened carefully, was polite and respectful to the teacher, kept persisting and went like a lunatic on the lung-busting 'freestyle' sessions. Perhaps some of that might rub off somewhere.

I would also suggest one of the principles of microadventures: if an idea sounds too daunting, do a smaller version of it. Go smaller and smaller until you find something you can all begin together. Some adventure always trumps no adventure. From that comes momentum, confidence and – eventually – a habit of trying to live more adventurously every day.

Young people are almost certainly more able to take adventures in their stride than you are. Don't underestimate them. Kids are bolder, more curious, enthusiastic, flexible, resilient, daft and up for new experiences than most adults I know. Pack lots of warm gear and snacks, allow plenty of time, and they'll rise to the challenge.

At some point, you will need to allow your little darlings to fly the nest, to take risks and be themselves. I have met many people who regretted *not* going on a big adventure, but I have never met someone who regretted going on an adventure. To stifle a young person's bold dreams is not caring for them; it is holding them back. You've done your job, and now it is time for them to put all your lessons into practice and to soar.

WHAT WERE SOME CHILDHOOD INSPIRATIONS FOR LIVING AN ADVENTUROUS LIFE?

I grew up in the countryside, enjoyed playing outside without adult supervision and went to a school that encouraged outdoor pursuits. As a teenager, we wandered around the Welsh mountains in small groups of six, smoking illicit cigarettes, getting lost and having a whale of a time in the rain (at least, I did; others detested it). All these factors influenced me a bit. But I had no inclination to do anything unusually adventurous until my first year at university when I simultaneously discovered the world of adventure literature and the joys of ascetic suffering in the hill through the Territorial Army. That was the real beginning of me setting off in an adventurous direction, more influential than anything from my childhood.

WRITING

What tools do you use to write your books?

I write two different sorts of books; narratives about adventures I have already been on and books that require me to conjure up ideas then write them down.

The first category begins with a journey. And all good journeys start with a map. Even though I increasingly use digital maps for my trips, I still prefer planning on traditional paper maps to visualise, annotate and scribble.

Out on the trip, I record as much as I can every day in a notebook. This includes facts and figures, what's happened today, my thoughts and feelings, and an ephemera of bits and bobs I've seen along the way. I have no desire to go digital for this phase. Phones smash, notebooks bend. I also collect stuff along the way and tuck it into the pages of my diary: leaflets, postcards, scribbled directions or maps and anything that will jog my memory when I come to write it all down later.

Photography is also an essential part of my writing process. Pictures are valuable aide-memoires for writing, allowing me to describe a scene later on more faithfully than I can with memory alone. I often take a photo purely because I know it will be a helpful 'reminder shot' for my writing.

Once I am home from a trip, the first task in turning an adventure into a story is to type up all my diaries. It is laborious, but it combines two important jobs. It creates the first rough skeleton of a narrative which I will return to later and flesh out properly. It also gives my brain its first opportunity to begin thinking about the journey as a single entity and a coherent story. This is a very different beast to the million moments out there in the wind and the rain, hungry and lost, when I was living every moment chronologically and without reflection or perspective.

After this point, all my books converge and are written in a similar way. They all take shape in my shed. Come in, take your shoes off and let me show you around.

My shed measures three and a half metres each way. It's a bog-standard garden centre cabin, with added double glazing, insulation, electricity and internet. Outside is a log for me to sit on and write when the sun is shining. One wall of the shed is all windows and glass doors, giving me a nice view of trees and bird feeders.

Another wall is taken up with a full-length desk, of which about half is raised to standing desk height. When I first experimented with a standing desk, I made one out of a plank and two piles of books. At first, my back ached, my calves hurt, and I was exhausted by the end of the day. Yet these are the very reasons why I tried a standing desk: my body had become accustomed to sitting down. Sitting down kills thousands of people every year. I got used to standing after about two weeks, and it has helped my back pains considerably. I am a definite convert.

After I decided to commit to writing standing up, noting the improvement to my back, posture, and energy, I had a desk made by a carpenter. It is very basic, but it is large (five foot by three), and it is precisely the right height for me. I stand on a 'standing desk mat' (a cushioned, rubbery, knobbly mat), which does a surprisingly good job of reducing the fatigue of standing all day. I recently revolutionised my winter mornings and announced my slide into middle age by buying a heated pad to stand on and keep my feet warm. It solved a perennial problem of getting cold feet in my shed, even with a heater and my giant Christmas elf slippers.

Standing at my desk now, as I write this, I will talk you through my working set-up. To my left, by the windows, is a section of normal-height desk and a wooden stool. The theory is that I sit there and work whenever I want to be away from a computer and engage my brain. I enjoy doing that, but usually every inch of that desk is covered with books, open notepads and pieces of paper covered in ideas and lists. Lined up along the windowsill is a row of smooth pebbles, sea glass, acorns and an Action Man head that I've picked up along the way. I have one of those in-tray / out-tray thingies in a laughable hope that my life might ever be so efficient. I peer into it about once a year. I have a glass jar labelled 'One Day' in which I stuff all the Post-it note ideas that have lain around my desk for so long that their colours have faded and I have to accept I'm not going to get round to acting on them any time soon. I don't want to bin them, but nor do I want them cluttering my brain, so I shove them into the jar, ready for the day I finally run out of ideas.

There are a couple of dozen Post-it note reminders scattered around amongst the wireless keyboard and mouse on my standing desk. My laptop sits out of the way on a lower shelf, plugged into a 27-inch monitor, which is invaluable for editing photos and video. The keyboard and monitor help me keep a better ergonomic writing posture than tapping away on a laptop. My laptop gets continually backed up onto a hard drive with Time Machine, and I do another fortnightly back up onto a hard drive that lives in my house, not my shed.

Also on my desk is a pair of speakers, two desk lamps, a pot of pens and pencils, two dirty mugs, a collection of conkers and driftwood, a SAD lamp and a 'Jar of Awesome'. The Jar of Awesome is a ceramic money box. Every time something good happens or I think something positive, I jot it down on a scrap of paper and put it into the jar (this morning's entry, 'Dawn Chorus!'). I use it to train myself to be more appreciative of all the small good events that are happening right now in my life.

Underneath my desk (out of sight and out of mind), are a couple of shelves holding a jumble of stationery, tripods, microphones, hard drives, a printer (I always print out my writing to edit with a red pen) and an old beer box that I toss all my accounting paperwork and receipts into. Once a quarter, I cheerfully deposit the contents with my accountant.

I drink bucketfuls of tea and coffee when I'm working, though at least I've moved to decaf. I alternate between drinking Yorkshire Tea and coffee made with an Aeropress as it doesn't really require cleaning. My mugs tend to get pretty grimy, however. The one health upside is that I need to go for a regular pee break behind my shed and so can do some pull-ups on the bar I've hung from a tree there.

When I am working, I listen to BBC 6 Music on my radio in the mornings unless I need to concentrate, in which case I play classical music. At 1pm, I switch to BBC Radio 3 for the rest of the day unless I need to perk myself up, in which case I find something loud and fast on Spotify. The only exemption to these habits is when I need silence for maximum concentration or when there's a Test match on, and I'm glued to the cricket on Test Match Special all day.

Pinned to the back wall of my shed, above the kettle and the radio, is a massive map of the area I live, tacked together from 1:50,000 Ordnance Survey maps. I use it to plan ideas, and I annotate it with interesting places I have discovered. There is also a Habit Calendar which I mark with an X every time I tick off the daily task I'm trying to build into a habit. When the chart is complete, after 100 days, I cover the Xs with white stickers and begin again on something different. I have used it, for example, to commit to concentrated periods of daily writing, pull-ups, morning pages and meditation.

The final wall of the shed, behind me, is covered with books. They are jumbled on shelves along with a goldcrest nest, a framed dollar bill from busking in Vegas, the original chapter illustration from *My Midsummer Morning,* and a couple of souvenir number plates found beside the road in Iceland and the Middle East. My seemingly disorganised bookshelves are a tremendous help to me in formulating ideas and putting plans together. I have a terrible memory for the details of books, but I remember well the gist of books as well as their size and the design of their spine. Seeing them helps jog my memory and gets me thinking. I am forever plucking books from the shelves and piling them around the floor to help me connect thoughts and shape the direction of my writing. In the past year or so, I have started to read on a Kindle. Whilst it is a fabulous gadget, I have not worked out a way to incorporate those books into my cross-pollinating process.

Other features in my shed: a large, tacky, faux-antique globe that opens into a drinks cabinet, though wisely there are no bottles in there. A red ensign I found washed up on a beach. A climbing harness hangs on a hook by the door in case I get the urge to go and climb a scarier tree than usual. Most ridiculous of all, standing in the corner of the shed, is a six-foot poster of myself that makes me chuckle. It is a testament to the powers of Photoshop that I look incredibly rugged on there. (I feel the need to explain such narcissism. A brand I once worked with had some posters made to promote a new rain jacket in outdoor stores across Germany. I had no idea about this until one day I spotted myself in a Munich shop window. I found this hilarious and asked if I could have one. So there I stand, brooding and hunky, smouldering in the rain in the corner of my shed. I have to be very careful when positioning my camera for Zoom calls so that the person I'm speaking to cannot see such a ludicrous shrine to myself!)

One additional tool I use specifically for writing books is Scrivener. It is a programme similar to Word, except that it is straightforward to shuffle chapters around, chop and change paragraphs and go back through your revisions. At the start of writing each book, I begin a new folder for every chapter and scribble down as much as possible, regardless of how rubbish it might be at first. I also chop up all my typed diary entries and paste them into the appropriate chapters.

In the early stages of planning books, I spread long blank rolls of wallpaper lining paper and loads of coloured pens across the floor of my shed, kneel down and start sketching out elaborate mind maps. I sometimes use a whiteboard for mind maps too.

I take digital notes throughout the writing process using the Simplenote app on my phone when I'm out and about. I often have ideas when I'm in the gym, on a run or reading a book in the evening. Simplenote syncs automatically with my computer, so every time I open a new browser tab my list of notes appears as my home page.

I also tease out ideas using notebooks and pens. I have a big old green leather armchair that I like to sit in when scribbling in my notebooks, of which I always seem to have two or three on the go at any time. I definitely feel more cleverer and well-inspired to write proper good stuff when I have a fresh, excessively expensive Moleskine notebook and a smooth black Uniball pen or an OHTO Horizon ballpoint. If I get stuck with my writing, I sit down for half an hour with a coffee and a notebook to write a stream of consciousness flow. Somehow that process often seems to solidify into something helpful. At any one time, I also have half a dozen coloured Post-it note pads on the go. All hail to the humble sticky note for the hyperactive but disorganised mind.

And that's about all I need to write my books. Plus, of course, the two most essential tools: time and persistence.

HOW DO YOU MAKE YOUR PRESENTATIONS?

I use Keynote for making my talks but usually export the slideshow as PowerPoint for clients after first flattening the images to avoid fonts going cRaZy and checking whether the images need to be 4x3 or 16x9. Then I send it via www.WeTransfer.com so that the presentation can be installed on the event's computer in good time. I am cautious of using video clips in my presentations (especially clips that need audio) due to the exponentially higher chance of something going wrong. But when I do include them, I send the files separately (in addition to the embedded versions), converted to the correct format and resolution for the venue I'll be speaking at.

HOW ON EARTH DO YOU PACK LIGHT? I FIND IT HARD EVEN FOR A NIGHT AWAY.

'We must not think of the things we could do with, but only of the things that we can't do without.' – *Three Men in a Boat*. Wisdom for life, as well as for packing a rucksack.

What does the process of putting a book together actually look like?

I'll take this book as an example for outlining the process of creating a book. This one began with a year-long email newsletter series called The Working Adventurer. Each week or so, I'd take one question, chew it over on a bike ride, then jot down my thoughts in a café.

Once I had written all those (and listened to feedback from readers), I put the articles into Scrivener and worked to convert it into a coherent book. This took a couple of months to do.

Next comes editing. I tapped up a few volunteers to read some chapters and paid three editors to read the whole book and offer their feedback. I then spent another three months editing the book again, working on the structure and order, adding missing content and removing thousands of words that now felt superfluous.

Around this time, I had a conversation with a book designer about cover ideas. My first idea was to have an iceberg on the cover representing all the unseen work behind the scenes that goes into becoming a Working Adventurer. Jim Shannon, the designer, nudged me instead towards the idea of all the different things rattling around inside my head. Somehow we landed on the idea that a papercut artwork would work well. I began conversations with artist Anna Brones about creating that. Having established the design timings and budget, I returned to my manuscript. I was beginning to hate it by now. This is a good sign.

I know that the book is almost ready when I become heartily sick of printing the manuscript out, scrawling all over it in red ink then typing up my corrections, printing the manuscript out, scrawling all over it in red ink then typing up my corrections. By now, I am cursing the project, wishing I had never started it, and convinced that it is a terrible idea. I run the book through Grammarly, a computer programme that helps check my speling and grammer.

One final part of writing a book is amongst my favourite bits: I print the book out, one chapter per page. Then I clear the floor and lay it out into sections. I walk over the pages looking for patterns, imbalance and inconsistency. Even though I know the book so well by now, this novel and different viewpoint always reveals things to me.

Ask An Adventurer is the 13th book that I have written, and each one has finished in the same way. I wake up one morning and can no longer face any more editing or proofreading. I do not care anymore. I am done. The book is done. I send the manuscript off to the designer and open a beer in the sunshine. Meanwhile, he gets to work laying out the book, making it look good in both paper and Kindle formats.

The design phase gives me some spare time to head to an audio studio to record the audiobook version of the book. Reading the book aloud, slowly, over a day or two hopefully reassures me that the book is not too bad. But it inevitably highlights some errors that escaped me in the countless edits. I send these to the designer, grovelling, begging him to fix them in the final layout.

With a traditionally published book, all of these stages would require collaboration and meetings with staff from the publishers. As this book is self-published, I can just get on and do most tasks myself immediately. If anything is wrong with this book in any way at all, it is my fault alone. But at least it all happens quickly.

On the plus side, once the book is ready, it can be published. Traditionally published books have a maddening lead time of many, many months between writing 'The End' and the book hitting the shelves.

Because this is a self-published book, ebook and audiobook (all via the Amazon behemoth), the final stage is to upload the text files and cover artwork to Amazon's Kindle Direct Publishing. I choose the categories I want Amazon to list the book under, add the ISBN number, pick a price point, and click 'go'. Boom! The book is available for anyone in the world to buy. As simple as that.

I have a celebratory cup of tea, go for a bike ride, and then start writing something else. (And, of course, begin the time consuming, exhausting process of marketing the book and drumming up readers. You could help, if you like, by posting a photo of the cover on your social media right now… Thank you!)

WHAT IS THE BIGGEST CHALLENGE YOU HOPE TO FACE IN THE FUTURE?

'All men's miseries derive from not being able to sit in a quiet room alone.'

How do I get my book published?

Most people who ask 'how do I get published?' are asking the wrong question. I believe there is a more important question to ask first. Before asking, '*How* do I get a book published?' you should ask, '*Why* do I want to get a book published?'

For example, I do not think these are good reasons:

- '*To get rich!*' The average full-time writer earns only £5.73 per hour.
- '*To get famous!*' If you're looking to build an audience, it is often easier and more effective to reverse-engineer a tribe through story-telling in other media, then write the book for that tribe.
- '*It sounds cool to have written a book!*' UK publishers release more than 20 new titles every hour. It is not an easy whim to indulge.

Here are some better reasons for wanting to publish a book:

- Because you have good ideas to share.
- To solve a problem in people's lives.
- To cement your expertise and authority in your niche.
- To tell your story for the grandkids. (Skip this chapter and go ahead and self-publish your book. It will be a lovely project to have completed.)
- You've always wanted to write a book. That was the end goal for me, at first. If writing a book is reward enough in itself, then all you need to do is apply the seat of your trousers to a chair, get on with it and then self-publish your work at the end.

Here are a few more questions to consider before committing to writing a book. (I know this book is supposed to be where I answer your questions rather than the other way round.)

- Do you want to *write* a book, or do you want to *have written* a book? This goes to the heart of the old noun/verb conundrum: so often we want to be the noun (a Writer) without grafting at the verb (actually writing).

- Do you really want to write a book, or have you just been on a marvellous adventure and a book feels like the thing to do?
- Do people often say 'you should write a book'?
- Do they still say that after reading a few of your sample pages?
- Do you really, really want to write a book? In terms of finance, time and frustration, the difference between telling a story and writing a book is similar to someone loving a meal you cook and then suggesting you go flip burgers for long hours and little pay or public approval for a year or more.
- Do you have any talent, training, experience or knack for story-telling? I have never had any formal training beyond the boredom of English GCSE, but I had written a blog for four years and told my story to hundreds of audiences before writing a book. I had also read countless books from my genre. That all helped. Bluntly, are you boring to listen to in the pub?

A fair few people who have been on fabulous adventures send me their manuscripts. Let me put this really politely... almost all of them are awful. Multiply this experience by a lot, and you'll get an idea of the vast slush piles of manuscripts and desperate cover letters covering publishers' desks. 'Dear Sir or Madam, will you read my book? It took me years to write, will you take a look?'

Before you dive too deeply into your writing dreams, send a couple of chapters of your work to some discerning, candid friends and ask for their honest opinions. Bear in mind when you do this that you're asking for a sizeable chunk of their time: ask for help, yes, but don't impose yourself to be helped. (On which note, please don't ask me to read your manuscript. I feel churlish saying, 'No,' and I feel a clot saying, 'Yes,' and then regretting it.) Will your test readers look you in the eye and urge you to keep writing? Or do they politely suggest you should look for other ways to tell your story or channel your creative energies?

Hopefully, these cautionary paragraphs have weeded out those who realise that publishing a book is not for them after all. However, if you are now clearer about why you want to be published, then the labyrinth of how to do it becomes simpler to navigate.

The short answer on how to get published (he says, 750 words into this chapter) is to spend a few days immersed in www. TheCreativePenn.com. Joanna answers all the questions about getting published with more expertise, enthusiasm and thoroughness than I can muster. Her books are well worth reading if you want to get published or earn money from your writing (not necessarily the same thing).

You need to think about several issues: whether you want traditional publication via a literary agent or without one; publication with a large publisher or a small outfit; to self-publish on Amazon, pay for a vanity publisher or crowdfund your book (perhaps with Unbound, a sort of hybrid between traditional and independent publishing). There are pros and cons of each route, except the paid vanity publisher option, which is totally unnecessary these days.

Finding an agent is often the first gatekeeper standing in your way. If you are not blessed with fortuitous connections or literary genius, there is no simple shortcut to finding a good agent. I consider it the equal of finding a publisher in terms of difficulty. There are masses of online articles about finding an agent, and working through a copy of the *Writers and Artists Yearbook* will also be time well-spent.

If you are writing a fiction book, the agent will want to read a polished finished copy of your sample chapters and cover letter. For non-fiction books, they will require a substantial written proposal for the book.

Most major publishers will only deal with you via an agent. Some specialist publishers, such as Summersdale or Vertebrate, do accept direct submissions. Their websites detail their requirements. You face very slim odds when trying to find a publisher, so don't make it even harder by sending your file in the wrong format. And a generic cover letter is the fastest route to an instant delete.

With my first book, I failed to find either an agent or a publisher. I was disappointed and envious of those who had succeeded. I felt hard done by. All that hard work wasted. I almost gave up on my book altogether. Fortunately, a friend persuaded me to consider self-publishing. My first thought was that this was only an option for losers who had failed to find a publisher and that I was obviously not one of those sorry types. But I gradually became more optimistic as I learned about the potential positives of doing everything myself.

Self-publishing via Amazon's KDP programme requires zero financial risk or outlay. They print each copy of your book on-demand, saving you from gambling on ordering thousands of copies that end up gathering dust once you have given all your friends and family multiple copies over consecutive birthdays and Christmases. You need not be daunted by how 'small' you or your story is. The Amazon page for your book will be the same as every other author's. Amazon subtracts its printing costs from the cover price, then gives you a share of the profit, typically a far more significant percentage than any traditional publisher will offer. It is a straightforward, democratic way to get published.

My self-published book sold 4000 copies in its first year via my website, my logistical operations hub (the back bedroom) and Amazon. This was sufficient to attract the notice of a small publisher who signed me up for my next few books.

Since then, I have experienced publishing with both small and large publishers, with and without an agent, and through self-publishing. There are pros and cons to each avenue.

- With an agent: you partner with an expert who will help get a good deal from a publisher. Agents understand the market and can help guide the direction and structure of your book. An agent can be an experienced ally to have on your side. Yet finding a good agent is hard, and they take the fate of your book largely out of your hands. You also have to pay a commission to the agent.
- Without an agent: you save yourself the agent's commission, typically 15% of all the money your book makes. Over time this hopefully amounts to a considerable sum. However, you miss out on their expertise and network of contacts for finding a publisher in the first place.
- A small publisher: it is easier to get your book accepted by a small publisher than a large one. You are more likely to receive a decent share of the editorial team's time and effort, but your book may end up with a relatively small print run and little marketing or publicity.
- A large publisher: you have a greater chance of seeing your book stocked in bookshops, as well as getting newspaper reviews and

marketing publicity. Hopefully, you will work with a higher calibre of editor and designer, though I have often been disappointed with chaotic working processes. I like the ego boost of casually saying, 'I'm with Harper Collins'. I won't deny that feels lovely and makes me proud. Yet you are only a tiny cog in a giant machine, and the publisher may forget your book after release. It is also harder to get your book accepted in the first place by a major publisher.

- Self-publishing: You are your own boss and will earn the highest percentage possible for each book sold. It is also the swiftest and surest way of getting your book published. On the other hand, you have no editorial or marketing support. It will be up to you to ensure that the book sells. It is unlikely to be stocked in bookshops, and production quality is still not as good as traditional publishing. This is definitely true for photo-heavy books such as *Microadventures* and *Grand Adventures* and illustrated children's books like *Great Adventurers*.

Nowadays, I mostly choose to self-publish my books even though I do have the option of using a traditional publisher. I do this mainly because I have built up a decent audience through my newsletters and social media. If I had no audience, I would prefer a traditional publisher. I now consider self-publishing to be my default choice for getting my books out into the world unless there are case-specific reasons not to do so. I self-published this book you are reading, paying freelance editors and designers to help put it together. I like the speed of process (up to a year quicker), control of the process, freedom of choice and higher royalties (60% of the cover price after printing costs versus 10% minus the agent's commission). It is also incredibly liberating to begin writing a book knowing that it will definitely be published. When I wrote my first book, I had no guarantee that my hundreds of hours of work would ever see the light of day.

The downside of self-publishing is that you need to hire your own editor, cover designer and arrange audiobook recording sessions. You need to be your own publicist and administrator. It is up to you to find an audience for your book and persuade them to buy it, so the audience you have already built becomes vital. I learned a lot about getting your book up the Amazon charts once I realised that publishers do negligible amounts of that stuff for non-A-List authors like me. Personally, none of these are downsides. I enjoy choosing who I work with and on what timeframe, and I have always made more effort to market my books than any publishers have.

Above all, I love that self-publishing means that I can indulge my stupid experimental ideas that traditional publishers would roll their eyes at. For example, I had an idea to write a blog post every fortnight, put it out as a newsletter and then, at the end of the year, turn all those articles into a book and try to sell it to the same audience who had already read the articles. It sounds daft, but the result of that experiment is the book you are reading now.

On another occasion, I was bemoaning that writing books is tough; there are so many pages to fill... So I began selling virtually blank notebooks on Amazon! It was a low-risk experiment. It cost me very little but now adds to my trickle of annual passive income streams.

So long as you can bear getting into bed with the Amazon beast, self-publishing is an excellent system for authors at all stages of their careers. You'd have to be a very dedicated anti-capitalist not to sell your books on Amazon. I also make my books available on Ingram Spark so that high street bookshops and websites like www.BookDepository.com and www.Bookshop.org can stock my books too. This means that all of my books are available to audiences worldwide.

I actually feel that, for now, Amazon treats writers more reasonably than the traditional publishing model does. I am aware that Amazon could change the way they operate overnight with zero regard for crushing authors like me. It is a gamble I am willing to take. After all, traditional publishing is, sadly, a gamble on a slow, non-agile industry tied tightly to physical high street bookshops. At least I maintain all the intellectual property rights for my work when I self-publish. I can change direction later if I choose.

In conclusion, ask yourself *why* you want to publish a book before mulling over the different options of *how* to publish a book. Re-read a dozen books you'd like to aspire towards in your writing. And then comes the critical part: write, write, write. Worry about the later phases of getting published much later down the line.

AS A WRITER, WHICH BOOK ARE YOU MOST PROUD OF? AS AN ADVENTURER, WHICH BOOK ARE YOU MOST PROUD OF?

As a writer, I am proud of *There Are Other Rivers*, my India book. It was a big creative step (breaking the journey down into a single day, with two threads – the journey and why I travel – hopefully melding together). But I would choose my Spain book, *My Midsummer Morning*, if I had to hold one up and say, 'This is my best effort at writing well.'

As an adventurer, I'd pick *Microadventures*. I think it has the most longevity and has actually encouraged people to go on adventures.

Do you have any tips for improving my writing skills?

The most significant gains in improving your writing skills come from two simple strategies: read a lot and write a lot.

The internet is full of lists offering 10 Quick Tips To Be A Better Writer, but it is important to realise that there are no shortcuts or lifehacks to writing well. There is a lifetime of learning to be had. I wish I had studied literature or creative writing at university rather than monitoring coots swimming on a pond in the rain. The writing course described by George Saunders in his book *A Swim in a Pond in the Rain* highlights what a writing naif I am and how ill-qualified I am to offer advice. But regardless of your qualifications, reading widely will improve your output. Writing in a public place where readers can respond and critique what you have to say will also be time well spent. (Go on: open up www.Medium.com and share some words with the world today. Publish a 2000 word post every week, and after a year you will have finished the first draft of a book.)

The temptation to spend time pootling through happy 'research' about pens and writing tips without achieving very much is the same diverting procrastination that sees folk scrolling endlessly through social media posts about getting fit or losing weight. We do not need more information. We all know what to do: eat better and move more. Sadly, broccoli and burpees are hard work, so we don't bother despite how much we yearn for the six-pack or published book. It is easier to read books on 'how to be a writer' than to dust off a pad of paper, grab a biro and be a writer.

However, if you want some practical advice from experts on the writing craft, I recommend the following books. Perhaps also sneak a dip into the archives of 70 years of author interviews by the Paris Review. They are available online or collated in the *Writers at Work* books.

- *A Memoir of the Craft* by Stephen King.
- *Bird by Bird: Instructions on Writing and Life* by Anne Lamott, which is worth the price merely for her advice on your inevitable 'shitty first draft' and the permission that gives you to begin.

- *A Swim in a Pond in the Rain* by George Saunders.
- *Save the Cat!* by Blake Snyder.

Revisit books that have moved you in the past, particularly those written in a similar style to yours. What sort of books resonate with you? Think about what writing style they use. Why is it effective? How do they do it? What do those writers do a lot of and what do they leave out? Think also about your natural tone of voice. When you speak about a subject, are you earnest and informative? Do you explain ideas well? Or are you frivolous or funny?

Note that the sort of book you aspire to write might not be what emerges when you put pen to paper. When I first began trying to write about my travels as a student, I wanted to write like Bill Bryson. I soon had to concede that my writing was simply not very amusing.

If this does not teach you enough to begin (pro tip: it ought to), then there are also a world of podcasts to help you find your writer's muse: How Writers Write, Monocle 24: Meet the Writers, Writer's Routine, In Writing with Hattie Crissell, Rule of Three, The Writer Files, The Creative Penn Podcast and many more.

But trust me on the 'read more, write more' approach to improving as a writer, even though it is not a quick fix.

HAVE YOU EVER CONSIDERED WRITING FICTION?

I would love to write a fiction book. It is high on my list of ambitions. The trouble is that I can never think of any good ideas. My chronic lack of imagination is part of why I have to go on long, often miserable adventures just so that I'll have something to write about when I come home. Also, when I read superb fiction, I regularly accept that the writer is operating far above my skill levels of observation, empathy and imagination.

But I have not discounted it altogether, and I definitely harbour plans to write a fiction book one day, if only for my own satisfaction at completing the challenge.

How many books do you aim to read a year? Also, are you ever overwhelmed by the sheer number of books that pique your interest and does it scare you that you'll never get to read everything you wanted to?

I don't have any aims for reading books. I just enjoy reading and enjoy learning from reading. Therefore I tend to read a lot. We all make time for what we prioritise. I carry a Kindle in my pocket and have the Kindle app and Instapaper app. (A bonus shout-out also for Readwise that helps you get the most out of what you read on your Kindle.) I can read for five minutes in queues or ten minutes while waiting for a friend. I read in bed, read when I eat meals alone, read rather than watching crap TV. These snippets all add up to me reading a book or two every week.

The sheer number of good books out there excites me rather than overwhelms me. But it does make me very harsh about quitting bad books early. I never slog through a book just because I've read a chunk of it already. A pilot only cares about the length of the runway ahead, not how much lies behind. Kindles are brilliant for this. I read many free sample chapters and don't bother with the whole book if it does not grip me.

My friends and family often ask to read the book I am writing, but I am scared to show them. How do you build the confidence to show people your work?

I love asking people to read drafts of my books and give me feedback. It is an enormously helpful process for a writer. When it comes to a finished book, however, I am much more nervous. I worry that readers will hate it or, worse, be indifferent. Publishing your personal writing leaves you very vulnerable. The thought of that scorn motivates me to show my unfinished work to people and ask for help. Their insights will improve the finished piece. I specifically ask for harsh criticism and boast of being 'unoffendable'. My editor described one chapter of this book as 'long and yawnsome'. That is a magnificent insult and one that I was delighted to receive, for it gave me a fighting chance of fixing the chapter before it was too late. You might still be finding this book long and yawnsome, but I promise you it is far better than it was thanks to blunt but well-meaning criticism.

The old military aphorism 'train hard, fight easy' is at the core of showing your work. Your writing is going to be criticised at some point. Better that it comes as early in the process as possible. Your friends and family will be sympathetic and kind, I'm sure of it. You'll probably find that it is hard to get them to say anything mean about your work at all. You must push for constructive criticism as it is invaluable in improving your writing. Before publishing, you need to reach a point where you are happy with your work, satisfied that it is your best effort and that your writing is honest and true, whilst also accepting that it's not as good as Shakespeare and some people will criticise you for that.

I would love all the feedback on my writing to be full of praise. Yet I know that my books are not the best books ever written. I understand that some readers will hate them and many more will quit halfway through. Criticism stings, but if you are preparing to write for the public, you will have to get used to it. Look at the online reviews of history's most significant books, and you will find hundreds of disgusted one-star reviews. But I am not writing this book for everyone; I'm writing it for a tiny niche tribe of folk who I hope will find it helpful.

Bear in mind that whilst it might be nice to invite your grandmother to be one of your early readers because it will make her happy and she has time on her hands, you will be better off seeking readers who are perceptive, thoughtful and read a lot themselves. (If that sounds like Granny, perfect.) Be prepared that some of the feedback you receive will probably be diametrically opposed in its suggestions. I never mind this as it allows me to consider different approaches before choosing the direction I prefer.

The public arena may slaughter your darling masterpiece. Armchair critics and vicious keyboard warriors hide uncaringly behind their anonymity. So you should be brave now and turn to those who have your best interests at heart and will help you all they can. Tackle the tabby cat to escape the tiger. Be grateful for all the feedback you can muster whilst you are still able to modify your manuscript. Train hard, fight easy.

WHAT IS IT THAT MAKES YOU CHOOSE TO DO SOMETHING DESPITE IT MAKING YOU FEEL VULNERABLE?

Over time, experience has shown me that it's good to do things because they make me vulnerable, not despite the fact. It is the route to growth, self-confidence, surprising yourself and a more interesting life.

Start with something small, reflect on how good you feel after it turned out OK and whether you'd like to try something similar again. Then repeat.

SPEAKING

How did you go about getting your first speaking gig?

I would like my account of getting a first speaking gig to begin with my oft-repeated trope that you need not worry about matters like this until you've gone off and done something interesting first.

But that's not how I went about it! My first talk took place a few days before I had anything interesting to talk about, before I had done anything at all.

My mum assembled her local WI group in our living room at home to hear all about the marvellous bicycle ride around the world that her darling son had not yet begun. I was embarrassed and at a loss over what on earth to talk about, but I figured that going ahead with the talk would pretty much repay 24 years of free rent and food, so I scampered up to my bedroom to take the world map off my wall whilst Mum made tea and sandwiches. I used drawing pins and string to approximate my imagined heroic route around the world on the map, manoeuvred my shiny new bike and panniers in front of the mantlepiece and began nervously winging it.

Clearly, it helps to have something interesting to talk about before you become a speaker. Failing that, there's nothing you can do about being a beginner except to make the best of things. 'Never be afraid to try something new. Remember, amateurs built the Ark; professionals built the Titanic.'

I had no intention of becoming a 'motivational speaker'. I'm not sure I even knew such a bizarre creature existed. But I did want to raise funds and awareness for the charity Hope and Homes for Children and so needed to tell my story somehow. When I pedalled into Istanbul, a school invited me to give a talk in return for a donation to the charity. The idea had never occurred to me, but I agreed, and the next 20 years of my life began.

I got that first school talk because a friend of one of my mum's friends' daughters lived in Istanbul, let me stay at their home, and her child attended the school. When getting started, you need to accept whatever opportunities come your way. Personal links, however tenuous, are invaluable for getting your toe in the door. Your useful network might not always be who you imagine it to be. I would suggest that you are thankful for any contacts you might have rather than resentful that you don't have as many as another speaker. That's a losing hand all of us can play.

I didn't yet have a lot to tell those school kids in Istanbul, though at least I now had two months' of tales from riding across Europe. I made my first ever PowerPoint slideshow, put my tent up for the kids, showed them my tiny camping stove and answered what would become very familiar questions about wild animals, favourite countries and going for a poo.

I ended up spending several days speaking to different classes. My presentations had to fit around the school's busy schedule. The slots varied from too short to too long, as they often tend to do in schools. Later on my ride, I cycled a considerable distance out of my way to speak at a school in Kenya and was then allotted five minutes to speak. More than once on that trip, a frazzled teacher saw me as light relief and sent me out in front of the lions for 90 minutes or more whilst they caught up on their marking or sneaked behind the bike sheds for a cigarette.

I didn't really mind what was thrown at me in the early years of giving talks. Each one was an opportunity to learn what an audience found interesting, then improve it next time. I'd try new styles, new approaches, new ways of telling old jokes. I began learning about the impact of pace or pausing, leaping around or sitting on a stool, galloping through a kaleidoscope of pictures or allowing one to linger. There are a million ways to give a good talk, but you need to give conscious thought to every detail you include or omit.

Over time I have settled on a personal preference of 30 minutes maximum for young children, 45 minutes for teenagers and one hour tops for adults, each with 25% of the time allocated for questions.

After the success of Istanbul, I decided to try to speak at more schools throughout my ride around the world. I spent many, many hours emailing schools asking if I could give a talk when I reached their city. Persuading schools to agree to my visit was a challenge I needed to think carefully about. A random guy emails and says, 'Hi, I haven't had a shower for months, a job for even longer. Occasionally I sleep in drainpipes under the road. Please can I come and talk to your pupils and encourage them to live like I do?' This was not going to be easy.

Schools are busy. Emails are a pestilence. Only a few teachers in a school have anything to do with organising outside visitors, if any at all. None of them knew anything about me. So I needed to strike carefully and precisely. Emailing a specific person rather than an info@school.com address massively boosts your chances of getting a reply. Getting those email addresses requires diligence, patience and networking skills. I pre-empted my spiel with something personal like:

'Dear Mr Oakenshield,
I was given your email address by your friend William Baggins. He told me about all your adventures together. I hope you don't mind me contacting you.'

I then explained that I was a qualified teacher to establish some credibility. I said I was cycling around the world to capture their interest and make this email seem different from the day's other dross. I quoted references from schools I had spoken at previously. I linked my adventures to one or two specific educational aims and asked whether I could share these experiences at their school.

I did all this in a succinct paragraph. You have time later in an email to point out relevant learning goals from the curriculum, mention money, clarify who you are and lay out what your visit to the school might look like in more detail. But you only have a few seconds of someone's attention when they open an email before they hit Delete. Whenever I gave a talk, I would ask teachers if they could personally connect me with any other schools along my route. I also made sure to collect a reference from every school I visited. This pursuit of references and word of mouth recommendations is critical and continues to this day, two decades after my first talk. Don't underestimate the power of a good reference. I began building my credibility and 'client list' right away and kept tweaking it as the calibre of my talks improved. Whether it is collecting speaker feedback, asking my audience to review my books and podcasts or forward a newsletter to a friend, every aspect of becoming a viable Working Adventurer benefits from asking others to take action on my behalf. It is up to me to offer sufficient in return for this not to feel irritating or parasitical.

(By the way, if you are enjoying this book, please leave a quick review on Amazon, post a photo of the book on social media or tell a couple of your friends about it... Thank you!)

I continued repeating all this for the next four years, giving over 300 unpaid talks on five continents. In return, I raised funds for the charity and often received bed and breakfast as well. Speaking at schools became a wonderful way for me to make quick friends in new cities. The hospitality and friendship of so many school communities was amongst my favourite parts of the whole adventure.

One of the best moments came when I returned to that first school in Istanbul on the homeward leg of my ride to give another talk. A teenager came up to me after my discussion and said, 'When I was a little kid, years ago, some guy came to speak to us about riding around the world. He was just getting started. I loved the talk and have often thought about it since. I wonder what happened to him...?'

WHAT DO YOU TALK ABOUT?

The content of each talk varies according to the requirements of the event. But I can generalise the rough layout of most of my talks.

I begin by trying to establish some credibility for the key points I will want to make later on. I explain who I am with some hopefully entertaining ripping yarns about a few of my bigger adventures. I talk about the lessons I learned from them and the directions my life has travelled as a result of them. I gradually start to incorporate some wider metaphors into these anecdotes. As I progress, these become more specific to the audience and the purpose of the event.

Finally, I end with some clear conclusions and calls to action. I get one bonus point for finishing punctually and a few more every time I make someone laugh.

How do you get paid to give talks?

When I decided that I wanted to give talks as a way to earn money and sell books, I began giving free talks in my village hall, nearby towns (on the back of a few local newspaper and radio interviews) and schools in my area. They helped me improve as a speaker and start spreading the word about my talks. Next, I moved onto speaking for free at schools via teachers I knew, in exchange for references and recommendations of other schools to contact. I also joined Speakers for Schools to talk to classes which was enjoyable and good practice.

I improved the content of my slideshows, polishing the content and improving the design. Over time, my anecdotes improved, as did the tone and focus of my delivery. I learned to tailor my talks to different age groups and the expectations of the audience. Are they here for entertainment or to be challenged and to learn?

The next phase was giving more talks at schools but now daring myself to be so arrogant as to request £50 for my presentation. It was a big hurdle for me to believe that my story was worth money and overcome my scruples to say, 'This is work. I ought to be paid for it.'

I sent out emails to schools seeking more bookings, gradually increasing my fee until I began meeting resistance. This is how you test your market value. It first happened at around the £200 mark, I recall. Your fee can increase again as your talks improve and your reputation grows. I found that private schools were more likely to have the flexibility of timetable to incorporate external speakers than a state school, as well as perhaps a tradition of such events. They also were more likely to have funds to pay a speaker, although even when I was giving talks for free I got more positive replies from private schools than state schools.

I also gave many talks at travel shows, cycling clubs, Rotary groups, and universities. These were often unpaid but helped me grow my audience. I sold quite a lot of books after these events, typically to about 20% of the attendees. Not only was this a good boost to my income, it also generated new readers, potential new followers and helped increase the number of people who knew about me (and might one day hire me for a talk, gift my book, or tell a friend in the pub about my newsletter).

I phoned up travel exhibitions at venues like Earl's Court and ExCel in London. I asked whether they had any unsold, unwanted, tiny, out of the way display stands that they might allow me to fill with my photographs, bicycle and charming sales patter. It would look better than an empty booth. My girlfriend sneakily printed out some of my photos in A3 on her office colour printer; I bought some Blutack and pedalled off to peddle myself. Those events were ridiculously exhausting and soul-destroying. I talked to an endless stream of passers-by about my adventures, handing out stacks of homemade flyers. I'm not sure those shows resulted in many talk bookings, but my attitude was that you never knew when you might get your lucky break. You've got to put yourself out there then hope for the best.

Slowly but steadily, my diary began to fill up, charging £400 for a talk now or £500 for a full day of talks. I learned that it is far better to speak only to a single year group rather than the entire school. If you talk to everyone, you won't be invited back for five years, but do an excellent job with Year Ten and you'll become a fixture in the annual calendar for years to come. There is, effectively, an infinite number of 'Year Tens' (or whatever age group appeals to you) across the country, and you could earn a fair living for life speaking only to them.

I had reached a point whereby I now had a sustainable income for as long as I was willing to tell the same tales over and over again. This is a key milestone for any Working Adventurer.

Speaking in schools is a brilliant, brutal education for a speaker. If you're bad or boring, then the kids will be sure to let you know! On the other hand, once you learn how to hold a classroom pin-drop silent, giving a keynote to a thousand executives is a piece of cake. You'd be surprised, also, how little you need to change the messaging or tone between the two groups.

My next stage was to progress onto corporate talks for the blunt reason that I could earn a lot more per talk. I began hustling speaking bureaus, trying to get signed onto their books. These bureaus help clients find speakers for their events. It is a crowded and competitive world. Most agencies already have a surfeit of adventurers on their books. But, with perseverance, I succeeded in getting a few speaking bureaus to take me on. I always tried to persuade someone from the agency to come and watch me speak. That is the best way of proving that you are good at what you do. All I had to do then was sit back and wait for the Ferraris to pile up in my driveway.

Sadly not, alas. Merely being on a bureau's books does not guarantee talks. Some bureaus have not found me a single booking in more than a decade, but as you don't have to pay anything up front, it is worth trying to get taken on.

Somehow, through luck, illness of another speaker or persistent pestering, an agency eventually puts you out for a talk. If you do that talk well, you might become flavour of the month and start getting multiple bookings from that agency. All is rosy until some young punk hustles their way in front of you in the pecking order, and the phone calls dry up once again.

In my case, getting established in corporate speaking mostly came from other avenues than the speaking bureaus. Cold calling never worked, nor did massive email mailshots. Word of mouth from other talks was vital, so I always preferred speaking to audiences of different companies rather than everyone from the same business. Parents who heard me speak at school events might book me to visit their company. Yet, most enquiries came via clients finding me online.

I began working with a speaking agent to help organise my talks. I have worked with Caroline for over a decade now, and it has been an excellent relationship. Caroline gets a fixed 20% slice of whatever pie she can negotiate for each talk and sorts out the stuff I'm terrible at (discussing money, negotiating contracts, gathering information I need before the briefing call, chasing deposits, etc.). Whether or not you decide to have a speaking agent will depend on how comfortable you are handling those matters. Personally, I'll hand over almost any pie to get out of paperwork, awkward conversations about money and the time-consuming detail of bookings that goes on behind the scenes. My speaking fees increased dramatically thanks to Caroline's friendly demeanour and canny experience.

I smartened up my website to look more professional. I made the Speaking page very prominent. I began a concerted mission to get myself placed high on the Google search page when someone typed in phrases like, 'Motivational speaker adventurer' (Number 2 on Google), or 'heroic, handsome speaker' (less successful). I spoke at a few events that I knew would produce a high-quality online video of my talk, for example, TEDx, The Do Lectures and The Lost Lectures. These videos would be helpful for clients to watch when deciding whether to hire me for their events.

As with all of my work, I preferred things being in my hands rather than in the hands of other gatekeepers. My website is one of the few areas I have total control over, a little bit of internet real estate all of my own. I spent years blogging regularly to build up content, establish a reputation, grow an audience, and make myself noticeable to anyone rummaging around for somebody suitable for their speaking event. I focused on topics that would be relevant and helpful for corporate teams. How could adventures be helpful, instructional or motivational for a school or business audience?

I repeated all these steps for many years and have finally become comfortably busy with speaking events. It sounds weird to me that I am now a professional 'motivational speaker'. It is a phrase that makes me cringe. Yet, when I do it well, it can feel like a worthwhile, useful craft to have dedicated myself to.

DO YOU EVER SPEAK FOR FREE?

I am often asked to speak for free. It is a conundrum faced by speakers, writers and photographers, yet not for some reason by dentists, electricians, farriers or anyone else with a job. Here is how I approach this issue.

By all means, do as many free talks as possible in the service of causes you care about: charities, Scout groups, whatever. For years I had a pro bono page on my website explaining that I gave 10% of my talks for free. This also helped me say, 'No,' with a clearer conscience to numerous requests.

Don't feel bad about declining invitations for unpaid work when they plead poverty yet come from ludicrously wealthy schools or businesses. I'd recommend sending a polite reply rather than the sarcastic, withering response you're tempted with.

Feel free to pass on invitations when the offer in return is 'good exposure' rather than payment. This is a really common way in which people try to get you to work for free. Yet do also consider speaking for free at events where there *will* be sufficiently good exposure to make it worth your while, if you need exposure at the time. For example, I am usually more inclined to do unpaid talks when the video will live for a long time on the web and reach a wide audience there.

Whenever you are speaking for free, look around the venue and ask yourself, 'Is anyone else here doing their best work for zero pay?' Are you being compensated sufficiently by the learning experience, the contacts or the audience? If not, you're a chump!

If you are still in doubt over what to do, consult the website www.ShouldIWorkForFree.com which will help you reach an appropriate decision.

I have been asked to talk at my child's school about an expedition I went on, but I'm terrified. Do you have any advice?

Fear of speaking in public, glossophobia, is apparently even more common than a fear of heights. I am often more nervous before speaking to an audience of children than adults and with good reason: losing control of an audience of youngsters is alarming and demoralising. (A quick tip: if they start chatting or fidgeting, don't try to talk more loudly. Instead, talk more quietly. Better still, stop talking altogether. Wait for their inevitable surprised silence, then continue.) Don't underestimate how hard it is to speak well for children. But also don't forget the joy of an interested audience, the impact of connecting deeply with children at a formative age and the exuberant delighted responses you may earn. You'll get more howls of delight, gasps of astonishment and whooping applause at a Monday morning assembly than at any corporate conference.

Don't waste this opportunity to inspire an audience desperate to do something unique with their lives. Someone in that room will never forget your visit. Quite probably it will be a young person who's not a traditional 'success' at school work. So make it good: that's a heck of a privilege and responsibility.

How can I improve my talks?

There are entire books about how to plan talks, and that is not really the remit of this one. So I'll limit myself to a few observations. If you want to read books on speaking well, I recommend *The Official TED Guide to Public Speaking*, *Taming Tigers*, *The Art of Asking*, *The Wealthy Speaker* (awful title, useful book), *Storyworthy*, *The Presentation Secrets of Steve Jobs*, *Public Speaking for Introverts* and *Slide:ology*. If you'd prefer a blog, dip into Nancy Duarte and Presentation Zen.

Above all, I'd recommend watching other people speak. Pay attention to what they do well and what feels phoney. There are so many good talks to watch online, whatever your interests. The TED archive is a perfect place to begin studying speakers. Search www. TED.com by topic, by recommendation or sheer weight of numbers. If overly-polished, overly-earnest Californians start to grate, head to a Welsh cowshed via www.TheDoLectures.com and start figuring out how to get from where you are to where you could be.

Planning a talk is not an easy process. I spent two solid weeks putting together a 20-minute talk for my session at The Do Lectures. Mark Twain allegedly wrote to Winston Churchill (or something like that) saying, 'I didn't have time to write a short letter, so I wrote a long one instead.' The same holds true for giving talks. After years of speaking, I could very easily stand up and blag an hour's talk with zero preparation, but crafting a compelling short speech is a fiendish exercise in paring away.

The best way to prepare for giving a long talk is by preparing for a short talk. If you can distil your thoughts into a Pecha Kucha format where you have just 20 slides that move on automatically every 20 seconds, then you are well-placed to do a full keynote. Pecha Kucha is my favourite format for both watching and giving talks. See www. bit.ly/NightOfAdventure for examples of talks from many Working Adventurers.

If you are uncertain about how to structure your presentation, I'd suggest planning to use most of your allotted time to share your adventures, failures and learnings. Keep a few minutes at the end for questions so that the audience can ask about what they really care about, not what you guess they might care about. This time is also a useful buffer in case you accidentally speak for longer than intended, which you are likely to do at first.

If you are nervous about the deafening silence of zero questions, prime a friendly audience member or two with questions to kick proceedings off. I have never given a talk where there were no questions at all, but I have occasionally had to cajole the first one out of someone to break the ice. In fact, I am always impressed by how many questions audiences do have. When I am an audience member, I have never dared to put my hand up and ask a question. I know that is weird when I am now quite accustomed to being on stage in front of everybody.

When planning your talk, consider that the audience has given up their valuable time to listen to you. What can you add to their day that a quick email would not do just as well? How can you help the audience? What are the key messages you wish to convey? Why are you giving this talk and not somebody else? How honest dare you be?

Once you have settled on your themes, begin to weave their thread subtly through your talk, building up to the critical closing message. Don't feel the need to say everything; stick to the stories that really get across your tale's essence. Telling stories is a good way to entertain the audience and convey memorable points simultaneously.

Be passionate, truthful and honest. Empathy always helps. Don't gloss over your struggles and triumphs. Do be self-deprecating and laugh at your own expense where appropriate. You can't have too much humour, so long as it is actually funny. If you are not a humorous person, do not try to be funny. Integrity is king.

Over time, the delivery of your anecdotes will improve. Pay close attention to the body language of the audience to decide which of your stories deserve expanding and which should be shelved. Similarly, treat the Q&A sessions like an invaluable Customer Feedback Survey. Notice what they are most interested in. Incorporate those aspects into your next talk. Axe even your most heroic, mock-humble yarns if nobody cares about them but you.

If you are unsure how to design your slides, go for a nice photo or even a blank slide with no more than one sentence of text on it (in a large, simple font) to jog your memory and prime the audience. Assume that the venue will have terrible visibility, so if you must have text on your slides, position it high up on the slide. Your audience will be savvy consumers of digital presentations and only too wary of death by PowerPoint. That means no Clipart. No pixelated images. No funny video clip of a kitten in a tree to start us off. No long lists of text swooshing with sound effects. No exceptions. It isn't 1997. If in doubt, heed Guy Kawaksaki's '10 20 30 rule', which suggests that no PowerPoint presentation should have more than ten slides, last for more than 20 minutes and contain any font smaller than 30 points.

Do not try to cram too much material into your talk. Less is more. Fewer slides is generally better. Regard them as prompts and titivation, not a crutch. Focus on having fewer take-home messages but making each one count. Remember that people seldom say, 'I wish that talk had been longer'.

Finally, the time to give your talk has arrived. You've practised in front of your bathroom mirror enough times. You know you've got the timings spot on and are confident with the narrative thread. Here are a few tips to help you deliver a better talk once you've taken a deep breath, checked your flies and stepped out smiling into the spotlight.

Make sure you know how to use the microphone and technology beforehand. You won't create a good impression by being bad at these basic skills.

Decide in advance exactly what your first sentence is going to be. This will remove the umm-ing and ahh-ing that often marks the start of talks. Nobody needs or remembers a rambling, wet beginning that takes two minutes to get going. Open with something solid and clear and relevant. The same applies to your closing sentence. It is the most important sentence of your whole talk. However much you ad-lib your material, don't fluff these key moments by leaving them to waffly chance.

Always speak clearly, make eye contact with people all around the room and smile when appropriate. Don't cower behind a lectern unless the event dictates that you have to. Move around the stage, but not in a manic caged animal kind of way. Show the audience your passion and your expertise, don't just tell them about it. Remember: you are on stage because you are the expert. You know more about your subject than the audience does (hopefully). They want you to do well, to entertain them and to teach them. Let that thought help you to relax and be confident.

Vary the pace throughout your talk. Without changes of pace and tone, an hour starts to feel like a long time. Be careful if you choose to accept questions during the talk. It is easy to lose your narrative thread or get interrupted by questions about topics you had planned to explain later on. I always prefer to take questions at the end.

Try to resist looking up at the screen all the time. It is depressing how often speakers give talks with their backs to the audience throughout. The most I ever do is cast a quick glance to check that the displayed photo still matches the story I am telling.

Remember the rule about having the minimum amount of text possible on each slide. Please don't have lists of bullet points which you then proceed to read out more slowly than I can read them in my head. You could have just emailed your presentation to me, and I'd read it at home in the bath, not in some shabby conference centre near a motorway junction. I know this is what everyone who has ever advised on speaking says. Yet it is also what happens at every single event I sit through. It sounds obvious, but speakers still do it, and it is soooo boring.

There are many factors involved in doing your job as a speaker well, beyond merely giving a good talk, so that your client feels happy and, hopefully, will book you again for future events. You need to build excellent interpersonal skills, focus on communication and empathy, understand what motivates different people and spend time building and managing relationships. These combine to help you create a reputation within the speaking circuit. Of course, your talks need to be consistently good, engaging and on brief. It is important to tailor them to specific and diverse audiences to ensure that you are relevant whilst remaining authentic. This requires listening carefully to a client's needs and asking pertinent questions. Organisers often struggle to articulate precisely what they hope to get out of their event. They know they want a good talk, but they don't know yet what that means nor how it amplifies their overall aims. How can you relate your stories to the audience's lives and professional situations in a non-cheesy, non-patronising, subtle way? You need to be honest, thoughtful and considerate. Your talk is not about you; it's about the audience.

You have to be ready to be flexible. I once had to slash an hour's talk down to 15 minutes on the fly thanks to the previous speaker over-running by 45 minutes. You also need not to be that clown of a speaker. It always gives me an evil villain shiver of delight when the speaker on stage before me is boring, corny or talks for too long. They are going to make me look great, so long as I don't make the same mistakes.

You need to pay close attention to the day's tone so that you can weave your story smoothly into the narrative of the whole event. I like to sit in on a few sessions before I am due on stage myself. You have to be able to read the room and pick up on the vibe. Does the audience want you to entertain, to inform or to inspire? Should you throw out some blunt home truths, or do they want you to make them laugh after hours of mind-numbing stuff about financial targets and redundancies? Do they just want you to hurry up so they can get to lunch?

You need to be friendly and sociable throughout the event, even though my preference would always be to hide in a corner reading a book. Although you are an 'external speaker', you know you have done your job well when delegates treat you as 'one of them' during the lunch break or evening drinks afterwards.

Above all, be passionate, be clear about your message and do not over-run. The old maxims are often true: Tell us what you are going to say. Say it. Tell us what you said. Sit down. The audience might like your talk, but they like the coffee break even more.

I WANT TO SWITCH CAREERS TO ADVENTURE PHOTOGRAPHY AND WRITING. WHERE DO I START?

1. Start taking photos and writing stories.
2. Practice, get good, build up an online portfolio. Teach yourself through YouTube videos, online courses or by going to night school.
3. Get known in your niche. Interact helpfully with those you admire on social media, blogs and forums. Share your work, tell people about it and seek out helpful criticism.
4. Do some work for free to build up your skills, portfolio and connections. The question of whether to work for free is a thorny one. But seeing as you already have a job, I'd countenance doing it here to help you get known more quickly.
5. Repeat 1-4 for as long as it takes, but with the vital difference of now charging as much as you can get away with. This figure will be small to begin with. Keep nudging it higher as your skills and reputation grow. You know you are charging too little when nobody questions your fee or tries to haggle it down. You know you are charging too much when the phone stops ringing. As a rough guide, my preference would be to keep the phone ringing all day. When it gets too busy, push your prices up.
6. Repeat until you have too much work to keep up your regular job. Drop down to four days a week, then three days a week until you are earning enough from your new work to be able to make the switch completely.
7. And now the hard work begins. Good luck. Enjoy it.

SOCIAL MEDIA

Was adventure better before the mobile internet?

I descended from a ferocious day of whiteouts, crampons, ice axes, bitter wind, and a beautiful white Arctic hare up on the Cairngorm plateau. Down for a hasty dip in a cold river, then into the peace of a mild spring evening in Aviemore. While I waited for the sleeper train back down to London, I headed to the pub. I sat down, had a few drinks and tried to recapture a little of what my adventures were like before the juggernaut of permanent connectivity came along. Every aspect of today's little adventure had benefited from a total lack of phone signal. What impact has mobile internet had on my more extensive adventures?

Before I launch into a misty-eyed rant about the good old days, let me be clear that I strived to be as high-tech as possible when I cycled around the world (from 2001 to 2005). I had my own website, which wasn't significantly different to an expedition website today. I had a one-megapixel digital camera which felt miraculous to use. 'Look on the back: that's you! I know, amazing, isn't it!' I was trying to tell as many people as I could about my ride and grow my audience whenever I found an internet café. I also used the internet as much as possible to sort out the logistics of the trip: finding embassy addresses to chase visas for wild countries, figuring out road conditions in rainy seasons and so on. The *Lonely Planet* 'On Your

Bike' forum was invaluable.

Cycling through Albania or Bolivia, I would have torn your arm off for today's connectivity. Worldwide WhatsApp? What's that? Internet on a phone? A *phone* on an adventure?! And it is also a camera and video camera? What is this sorcery?! Kindle books galore (compared to the ludicrous 27 books my friend Rob and I lugged through Japan on our bikes). A SPOT tracker in dodgy places. Google Maps (cycling into megacities like Cairo, Mexico City and Tokyo without online mapping was a palaver). Social media and a blog that I could update by myself from the road. All of these are invaluable to the aspiring adventurer. They keep your friends and family in touch. They connect you with like-minded folk and are helpful, useful, and often free. They are astonishing tools for telling the story of an adventure.

The internet has improved adventure in so many ways. It is much easier to plan expeditions and connect with experts before you begin. There were many more headaches, hassles and delays on my travels before phones with mobile internet connections became commonplace.

Communicating and expedition admin has never been easier than today. Consider the lads from the Bombay Weightlifting Club who cycled around the world in 1923. In *With Cyclists Around The World*, they wrote, 'we wired for a new cycle. But there was a strike of the Chinese workers and the telegram could not be dispatched.' Spare a thought for the logistical struggles of Heinz Stücke, who spent 50 years cycling around the world, amassing 100,000 analogue photos along the way. Today's global adventurers can order parts online, checkout via PayPal and be on their way again as soon as they've updated their Insta Stories on their phones.

On some expeditions, I have been more connected with the world than I would have liked. I learned that Whitney Houston had died when I was in the middle of the Atlantic Ocean. I was in a tent in Greenland when Sergio Aguero won the Premier League in the last minute. Contrast that to pedalling peacefully through a rainy German autumn without realising that 9/11 had rocked the world.

I prefer being distanced from the daily news cycle when I'm away. Huge news catches up with you at some point. Meanwhile, all the flash in the pan stories evaporate without worrying you or distracting you. It is a rare treat to escape all that sound and fury. It is why I put my phone onto Airplane mode, even on short microadventures, days in the hills or holidays. Huckleberry Finn felt the same freedom on his raft, 'So in two seconds away we went a-sliding down the river, and it did seem so good to be free again and all by ourselves on the big river, and nobody to bother us.'

Looking back, I am grateful for the total immersion that comes from being cut off from the outside world when you have no means of communication. It is possible to get this experience these days, but it requires self-discipline. I carried a 4G phone whilst busking through Spain but kept it offline. Years ago, you did not have such a choice to make. I used to send emails to my mum along the lines of 'I'm leaving Beijing in the morning. Don't worry if you don't hear from me until I reach Kazakhstan next month.'

In Africa, I remember a pick-up truck stopping to chat after I'd spent a couple of weeks hauling my bike along the sandy tracks of the Nubian desert. The driver mentioned that he had a computer in Khartoum. I scribbled my parents' email address on a scrap of paper and asked him to reassure them that I would be back online in a week or so when I emerged from the desert. He kindly passed on the message.

When I sailed across the Atlantic Ocean, nobody had any idea where I was until I called home from a payphone on a humid street busy with hawkers and taxis. 'I'm in Rio!' Later that night, a girl gently took my head in her hands and cut off 18-months of my curly hair, scissors in one hand, Caipirinha in the other, cigarette between her lips, cicadas and samba and the Southern Cross in the air. My hair fell at our feet, and it was the end of Africa and it was the beginning of the Americas. And it was the beginning and the end of the two of us; without WhatsApp to keep in touch, we faded like smoke rings from each others' lives.

In Patagonia, I heard rumour of a remote, alternative border crossing into Chile. The crossing was not open to vehicles and did not appear on my large-scale map (half of South America on one sheet of paper). It would require cross-country travel and a boat ride if, indeed, it even existed. I could not find out any detailed information. Even a helpful police station, after much noisy telephoning and gesticulation to their colleagues in other areas, could only advise me that 'there is no road and there are only two boats a month, perhaps around the 5th and the 20th'.

When I eventually arrived at the border post hut, the customs official pointed out a muddy path disappearing up the forested mountain and said, 'You want to get to Chile, *amigo*? Just follow the horse crap...'

After I crossed the pass and descended to the slate grey waters of the lake, dotted with blue icebergs, I did not know when, or even if, a boat would arrive. I had no Kindle or Instagram to kill time. Instead, the weight of time felt luxuriant, decadent and fascinating. I had a crossword puzzle, a book I'd picked up somewhere about the Pyramids, some tea bags and popcorn kernels. I spent many hours skimming stones across the lake in the silence.

The critical point of the before and after internet debate, I think, are the times like this when total disengagement with one world permits full engagement in the world and the experience that you are actually in.

Compare all that to the task of creating the daily social media stories that I shared whilst cycling around Yorkshire in 2019. So time-consuming was all the photo editing and posting that I didn't read a single book on that ride. Yet on other adventures, I had time to read *War and Peace* in Russia, *Atlas Shrugged* in California, *Anna Karenina* on the Arctic Ocean and so on. This is the luxury of time.

Spending an hour in an internet café was one of my favourite treats in my early travelling years. They were a tantalising hook to the outside world and home. Those ramshackle, pay as you go, backroom enterprises were my opportunity to tackle a few admin tasks on painfully slow dial-up connections. Whilst teenagers chain-smoked unfiltered cigarettes, listened to loud music through tinny speakers and cheerfully slaughtered each other in violent gun battles, I might arrange to ship a bottom bracket to a postal address a few months' ride away, confirm a school talk next month, grin at banter from a mate back home and hope for a message from a girl. You had to hurry to get everything done before your time was up or the electricity went off. Nostalgically, I even cherish the screeching dial tone when the routers needed resetting and the chug-chug-chug of the diesel generators keeping the lights on.

There were not so many adventurers tackling long haul rides back then. I knew of a few legends from forums and still remember their online nicknames; Corax, Tracksterman... Yet, I had no idea what they looked like or who they really were. You might know, say, that someone was riding from Europe to China and that you had a chance of intersecting at one of the bottleneck embassies in Central Asia. But you could not track their progress from day to day as you can now, so actually meeting was a lottery. Today, most expedition websites feature a live tracker showing a person's progress from hour to hour across oceans and ice caps for the dot-watching enjoyment of all the followers back home.

I cannot overstate the thrill of seeing a loaded bicycle approach down a long straight road after thousands of miles by yourself (and the disappointment when it turned out to be yet another donkey laden with water barrels). Or seeing a touring bike leant up outside a dusty adobe stall selling warm bottles of fizzy drink in a sleepy village somewhere far from a paved road. Those meetings and the excited babbling of news were perhaps my most significant connection in the five or so years of my life I spent on the road. 'I hear you. I understand you.' Empathy, sympathy, company. I wonder whether, overall, I was more or less lonely by being unconnected for so long?

I felt solitude, not loneliness, during the ten days on the high South American *altiplano* when the only soul I spoke to was my own, dragging my bike and equipment across the lunar landscape, oxygen-starved, spitting blood, wind-whipped. Nobody on earth knew where I was or could get in touch with me.

I have passed many nights weather-locked in my tent without the scrolling glow of Twitter to fill the void. I used to read and re-read a slim book of poetry to pass the time. Tent-bound in a snowstorm in China, I memorised a poem while the polluted smear of the city in the valley below was blanketed clean by falling snow. I read the lines out loud, over and over, accompanied by the noise of coal lorries sluicing through the slush,

'The sunlight on the garden
Hardens and grows cold,
We cannot cage the minute
Within its nets of gold.'

'Oh well,' I sighed, as the light faded and the snow continued to fall. 'At least I'll be able to get a new book when I reach Kazakhstan next month.'

Yet, I still think that this stripped-down existence is a richer form of adventure than having a phone filled with all its treasures of distraction in the tent with you.

DO YOU STILL HAVE ANY OF YOUR BIKES FROM THE BIG RIDE? IF SO, HOW DOES IT FEEL TO TOUCH THEM NOW?

I chucked my bike into the metal recycling section at our local tip years ago. I figured I didn't need a knackered old bike to remind me of the open road, especially as I deliberately didn't buy or collect a single souvenir in all those years. I loved the minimal simplicity of that life, so why would I clutter up my future life with 'stuff'?

(Counter argument to the minimalism: I also kind of wish I'd bought a painting in every country I have ever visited and now had a crazy, crammed, eclectic house.)

How has social media changed the way you tell your adventure stories?

If I was 24 today and about to set off around the world, I would embrace all the social media and mobile phone technology available. And yet, at the same time, I also hold the contradictory belief that I am glad to have done my ride without them.

If I was beginning to build a career in adventure, I would go for full connectivity. Much of your viability as a Working Adventurer depends upon the oxygen of publicity. You need to do interesting journeys, of course, but if nobody knows about them, you're not going to earn a living. You need to build, grow and hold onto an audience of supporters. Social media is spectacularly helpful for that.

Yet, by *not* having social media when I began, I had exceptionally rich experiences, which perhaps gave me a more solid platform to build a career in the long run. Who knows; it's all speculation and guesswork. But that hypothesis fits with the slow and steady approach to longevity I prefer to a sudden burst of social media attention that can disappear just as quickly.

If I was 44 today and about to set off around the world (and could afford to do so without earning money from the story en route), I would have zero social media or online presence. I would do it in the way I busked through Spain, carrying a phone to use the maps, Google research and WhatsApp my family, but with all the social apps and email removed.

It used to be that someone would go away on an adventure, scribble some notes and take a few photos. Then they returned home and tried to figure out how to tell their story and find an audience. Nowadays, there is pressure to do all these activities simultaneously and beautifully. There are obvious benefits for the freshness and immediacy of the story, but trying to do everything at once also risks not doing justice to any aspect of the experience. It is possible that our 'look at me' culture results in blander, shallower experiences because we are too busy seeking attention to pay attention. You benefit from a deeper immersion into nature and a fuller engagement with the adventure when you are not feeling the temptation or the distraction to put something on social media to impress others.

When I cycled the length of Africa, I wrote updates for my website in Cairo, Aswan, Khartoum, Addis Ababa, Nairobi, Moshi, Dar Es Salaam, Blantyre, Francistown, East London, and Cape Town. Just 11 updates from a year spent cycling the length of a continent. That's it! These days I sometimes post 11 Instagram Story updates in a day.

By the time I reached Cape Town, I had uploaded just nine photos to my website and had the temerity to thank Olympus at the top of the page for sponsoring me the camera! I'm not sure they got a great return on their investment. In my whole ride around the world, I only took 3425 photos. (I have taken that many on week-long adventures in recent times.) No wonder, perhaps, that I have never since managed to find sponsorship from a camera company.

There are a lot of decisions to make about using social media and the internet on your adventure. If an expedition has sponsors, then you are likely to be duty-bound to maximise your story-telling. Rowing the Atlantic, for example, we made sure to write a blog post every day and upload it via satellite phone from the middle of the ocean, even when (or perhaps especially when) we were all puking unhappily.

If you are on a long journey, such as crossing a continent, it makes sense to keep your audience interested by posting updates along the way. Whether that is once an hour or once a month is up to you. There are advantages and disadvantages either way.

Nowadays, I mostly go on short microadventures. I prefer to not worry about sharing anything online while I am away. I make the most of the trip. Afterwards, I make the most of the story by telling it more thoughtfully than I would if I was feeling pressured to Tweet whilst slogging through a storm or desperate to get some sleep.

Each social media platform works well, but differently, for sharing your adventures. Facebook, for example, was invaluable when I was trying to grow a community interested in microadventures: over 40 local groups formed to chat, plan and meet up and my Microadventures Page became my largest online channel.

Instagram is excellent for concise story-telling to a very engaged audience. Twitter is good for sharing information, testing ideas, finding answers to questions or posting short and regular updates. TikTok buzzes with potential for entertaining or educating.

YouTube is a brilliant place to share adventure experiences, whether through GoPro action footage, helpful instructional guides filmed on your phone or fully-fledged adventure films. Canny SEO labelling on YouTube is also an easy way to rocket you to the top of a Google search page.

The immediacy, democracy and vibrancy of all these superb tools makes this a brilliant era to be a Working Adventurer. Social media allows us to tell stories better than ever before, more efficiently and to a global audience. It is a tantalising opportunity. By contrast, the year-long, silent slog to write a book that might never get published or attract only half as many readers as an Instagram post seems completely crazy and antiquated.

Social media helps you grow an audience, as well as to build a reputation and a portfolio. These are good starting points for earning money to pay for future adventures. With all the tools available now, any young adventurer is so far ahead of where I was when I used to idle away long and empty miles with ludicrous fantasies of somehow becoming an author one day.

Yet now that I am a Working Adventurer, I feel I have got into bed with the social media devil and have to keep telling my stories: it is my job. (It is also, I suspect, a habit.) There are heart-warming occasions when someone tells me that their own adventures began because of my social media posts. Hopefully, in turn, their shared experiences will inspire others to hit the road too.

But, I also know that this comes at the cost of changing the experience itself, the experience which is supposed to be the point of the whole thing. Walking across the Empty Quarter desert was the first expedition I ever did where the story was more important to me than the journey itself. I revelled in a newfound obsession with camera angles, continuity shots and charging batteries with solar panels. I loved that adventure as much as any of my others. It was a rich and interesting experience. It was not worse or better than adventures where I did not need to stop and document every experience. But it was very different.

Social media story-telling has increased the vicarious enjoyment of adventures and made it a richer experience for the audience. It has become an integral part of the experience of being a Working

Adventurer. It is not necessarily better or worse than the olden days of ten years ago; it's just different. And you always have the choice to switch your phone off if you don't like it.

WHAT IS THE WORST FOOD YOU'VE EATEN?

Among my more memorable meals, you can pick from sheep's head, guinea pig, snake, crocodile, bear, fried worms and scorpions, sea urchin, raw squid, horse, strong Lebanese cheese, Japanese *natto*, Icelandic whale and far too many late-night Scottish kebabs. And I was once invited, as an honoured guest, to kill a pig for a feast by shoving a stick through its heart. The only thing I have been too squeamish to try was boiled mice on a stick in Malawi.

When did most of your social media growth happen?

I have never found a quick-fix solution to social media growth. Back when I used to keep an eagle eye on my website's stats, I would notice a traffic spike on days when I was interviewed on the radio or had an article in a newspaper. Unfortunately, I also saw that visitors would immediately drop off again afterwards and had zero impact on the quantity of books I sold or my regular numbers of readers.

I learned to spend less time chasing quick bursts of publicity and dedicate more time to slowly building a solid audience from the bottom up. Today's news is tomorrow's fish and chip wrapping.

It has been a similar tale with social media. On the rare occasions when a big name or publication mentions me, my numbers briefly jump up but quickly return to normal. I once gave a few talks for Pinterest, a popular platform that is brilliant for particular niches of creator, but not my core demographic. Because of the events and the publicity from them, I ended up with 140,000 Pinterest followers. But it is not an active and engaged 140,000 people and has not led to an increase in speaking assignments or book sales.

This highlights a giant difference between increasing your tally of followers versus increasing engaged followers. I know of several Working Adventurers who have bought tens of thousands of social media followers very cheaply. I would like to say that it is a pointless, vain thing to do, except that when brands look to work with influencers, they are obsessively drawn to the number of followers you have, regardless of whether they are true fans or the product of a far-off 'click farm' run like a massive call centre.

I have not been immune to the lure of numbers. Whilst I have never bought followers, I did go through a phase of boosting key Facebook posts using paid adverts in cheap regions of the world. I don't honestly think many Bangladeshi Facebook readers were very interested in my camping advice. Still, their numerous eyeballs made me look more popular than I really was, which did make me momentarily happier in a pathetic sort of way and made me more appealing to clients.

Another way to look at audience size is that there are only 'X' people in the world who are going to be interested in what I do. There's no point in envying a footballer or a mainstream famous adventurer because they are operating on different levels. All I can do is work hard to reach the audience who are going to be interested in what I do and be content with that number.

Overall, my social media growth has been gradual, but steady. Growth comes from consistently putting out regular, helpful content, engaging with the audience and connecting with relevant, related online communities to gain new, interested followers. Over time the benefits of compounding kick in bit by bit as more people tell more people about you or link to you in their social media posts.

As usual, there is no instant solution. If something looks too good to be true, it probably is. There really is no long-term alternative for growing a social media audience to plugging away, putting out the best stuff you're capable of doing and gently asking folk to follow along if they are interested.

(By the way, you can follow me on Instagram, YouTube, Twitter, Facebook, LinkedIn and, of course, Pinterest.)

THE MOST WELCOMING PEOPLE ARE FROM...? (NAME THREE PLACES FOR US.)

Syria, Sudan, Siberia.

How do you deal with answering emails and keeping on top of social media?

Today is a marvellous era to be a Working Adventurer. It is so easy to reach an audience who is interested in what you do. Partly for interest and partly out of blatant procrastination, I just checked to see which countries my newsletters are read in. There are almost a hundred. Hello, world!

As easy as it is for me to reach an audience, so too is it easy for that audience to contact me (hit 'reply' to one of those newsletters, and it zaps directly to me in my shed, wherever you are in the world). This is fantastic: it is helpful, informative and plain nice to hear from fellow adventurous souls who are interested in my work. Building steadily and concentrating on a loyal core audience is the mantra of Kevin Kelly's '1000 True Fans' thesis that I've based much of my working life on. Kevin suggests that if you can find a thousand fans who will buy everything you write and support everything you do, then you have the potential to build a viable business. You should not be discouraged by thinking that success can only come with a million fans. For years I worked hard to answer every email, every Facebook comment and every Tweet, growing my thousand one by one. I also did it to help those people, to be polite and to build relationships.

However, as the number of comments and emails grew and the breadth of social media platforms spread, my system eventually became unworkable. I could spend every day replying to emails, or I could write my next book. I could not do both. 'An inbox is a to-do list to which anyone in the world can add an item.'

And so, with reluctance, I began streamlining my communication. I say 'with reluctance' because it felt rude not to answer. But continuing to post content online whilst decreasing the ensuing dialogue is the only way I can actually get books written, which I consider to be my most important work. (I could, of course, stop doing everything except writing books, but I have not been successful enough as a writer to just drop a book a year and allow the screaming multitudes to do all the promotion work of their own accord.)

My solution to the communication dilemma has been to spend the most time engaging with those who have spent the most time connecting with me in the first place. For example, I made a blanket decision to ignore all Instagram and Facebook messages once I started getting too many to deal with. It took me a while to not feel like a rude diva about this. Yet it takes ten seconds for someone to write, 'Yo dude. Love your content! What equipment do I need to cross Greenland?' It would take me an hour to do justice to an answer. I opted not just to pick and choose the messages I reply to because I feel guilty and compelled to answer once I have seen a notification. So I make it easy for my brain by simply never looking at those channels. (That's my version of Obama wearing the same colour suit every day).

I do my best to answer all the emails I receive, though with brevity (and, I hope, gratitude). Turning frequently-asked questions into FAQ pages or blog posts is a helpful strategy, as well as a good source of writing ideas.

When it comes to defending my time, I try to cut people off at the pass. I want to be accessible, but I also want to be doing my work rather than being at everyone's beck and call. So the Contact page of my website links to my FAQs and blog posts that answer the majority of queries I receive. It then lists my agents to contact if the enquiry is about various strands of my work, with a link that addresses common requests from journalists. Next, I try to nudge someone to contact me via Twitter where I can reply quickly and promptly. Finally, I provide my email address in case none of this has solved the problem, and they want to email me directly.

I particularly appreciate automated Gmail Canned Responses for helping me say 'No' to invitations that guilt, wimpishness, greed or vanity make me inclined to say 'Yes' to. Saying 'No' more often is perhaps the number one magic trick for getting important stuff done, for freeing up time and mental space to do the important work. I find it helpful to have a series of pre-prepared canned responses in my emails. I click a button, and off it goes. I don't feel so bad about being unhelpful or disappointing someone this way. In case it may help you, this is what one of my messages says:

'Thank you very much for your kind invitation. Unfortunately, I am trying to buy back a little time in my life by saying 'No' to interesting opportunities that I'd ordinarily love to say 'Yes' to. Apologies not to be saying 'Yes' this time. I hope you'll understand.'

My approaches to tackling email come and go, but the essence is always about doing it in speedy batches, not drip by drip (except when I'm lazy and looking for excuses not to do proper work). Usually, I check email twice a day. When I get fed up with my working life, it becomes once a week. When I am procrastinating book writing, it becomes a pointless and pathetic once an hour. I dream of deleting my email account altogether, but I know that it is the gateway to much of my paid work. The day I retire, however, the email address is going. Even writing that sentence makes me smile.

Imagine your working life is an empty jar. Fill it first with the few large stones that are your priorities. You'll still be able to fit some pebbles into the jar around the edges. These are the other smaller but important tasks you need to get done. Finally, fill whatever gaps remain with sand. The sand is email and social media. If you make the mistake of doing it the other way round, putting sand into the jar first, you will have no space for your work's large stones.

When I email businesses or working people, I expect them to reply promptly. Not instantly, but within a few days. I've always given short shrift to the excuse of being too much of a hobo for email. On the other hand, don't let it steer your schedule or distract you from the genuine work that needs doing.

To keep organised and efficient, I schedule my life via Google Calendar and defend my time tightly. I block off non-negotiable chunks of time as early as possible (an hour per month to climb a tree, two days here to film a microadventure, a precious bigger chunk for a bigger adventure). Without doing this, time quickly gets fragmented by small commitments that break up substantial periods when I can tackle meaningful activities.

I try very hard to avoid meetings and do them as Zoom calls instead. I try very hard to avoid Zoom calls and do them as emails instead. I try very hard to make email exchanges brief and actionable.

If I do need to attend a meeting, I try to cluster a bunch of them together and then drink beer on the train home after a full and productive day. I like to ensure in advance that everyone at a meeting is aware of what we need to get out of it and then be clear what specifically needs doing afterwards, by whom, and by when. When I can't escape from phone calls or interviews, I batch them all on the same day if possible. Otherwise, I find they hang over me and distract me. I'm always surprised how much a single scheduled call in my calendar disrupts an entire writing day.

I use the Schedule Send function on Gmail to deal more efficiently with future tasks. For example, I uploaded every episode of my podcast many months in advance. At the same time, I scheduled a personal email to each podcast guest for the morning that their interview was released to thank them and provide the link to their episode, asking if they would be so kind as to share it with their audience too.

I do all boring stuff in batches: sending invoices (I use Debitoor for this), sorting out tax, putting together presentations, ordering book stock or buying train tickets. I hate those sessions. Doing everything myself is not smart, I know. With some aspects of my work, I suffer from the absurd delusion of thinking I can do everything better than everyone else. I am also too impatient to take the time to teach someone to help me with routine tasks. I'm also weirdly private for someone who spends a lot of time writing about himself. I don't like sharing the details of my life. I know that it would be helpful for me to change these foibles and work with someone who could help organise my working life.

I am getting better at delegation and really appreciate the collaborations I do have. I hired an intern a while ago to help me think differently. Unfortunately, she was so impressive that she quickly got head-hunted by a company that could pay much better than me.

I work with agents to manage my speaking enquiries, my work with brands and my publishing contracts. I also have an accountant, and I urge anyone who goes self-employed to spend their first paycheque on hiring an accountant. I wish I had done that. I spent my first paycheque on a gorilla costume. I'd urge you to spend your second paycheque on one of those. If you shoehorn the gorilla into every themed fancy dress party you are ever invited to, it will prove to be a sound investment.

A significant but time-consuming part of being a Working Adventurer is building a decent presence on social media across multiple platforms, adding content to your website and growing an email database. The key to this is regarding it all as work, not as a hassle or a bit of fun. I adopted this attitude when I realised that the only way I could make a living from adventure would be if people knew that I existed.

I began treating my blog like a part-time job, working hard to schedule regular blog posts month by month. I would sit down once a month and write several weeks' of content in one go. (The '31 Days to Build a Better Blog' course by ProBlogger was invaluable. I repeated it every six months for several years.)

Similarly, I consider social media as 'work' and keep my channels well-stocked with scheduled content. As well as writing my own material, I try to be a hub of relevant articles on Twitter, Facebook and LinkedIn. I read lots of articles and share the good ones. Instapaper's app and Chrome extension are helpful for doing the research efficiently at times that suit me. When I find good posts, I schedule them using www.Buffer.com, which spreads the content out rather than dumping lots of links online at one go. It also makes it very easy to post on multiple platforms. I build up a stockpile of articles so that one or two interesting links are shared every day, even when I'm not at the computer. I like to set up as much as possible to save myself from being stuck behind a computer. I often have social media posts organised for many months to come, with minimal effort.

I also schedule many of my Instagram posts in advance on top of posting more immediately when I do something relevant. I find it helpful to think thematically about the planned content. For example, I might decide to share a running photo every week with an anecdote to accompany each one. Rather than clogging my mind and To Do list for ages, I upload a batch of them using www.Later.com. Not only is Later efficient, but it also keeps me away from the Instagram app itself and all its distracting shiny bicycles and mountains that lure me away from my writing.

I often use the #tbt hashtag (Throwback Thursday) as an excuse to reshare old photos and stories. It's worth remembering that just because you did something years ago does not mean that the tales and lessons are not still relevant today. You will also have new followers who have not heard those stories before. Again, I schedule series of these posts a few months at a time.

Later is also helpful for spreading the story of an adventure out evenly. A few folk criticise me for 'making it look like you are adventuring all the time'. But I don't try to pretend that my adventures are longer and mightier than they are. I do make an effort to 'use' the stories efficiently. Imagine, for example, that I abseil off a big cliff, leap into an icy river and meet a kind stranger... all within ten minutes. I could post three fantastic pictures and stories within ten minutes. Or I could post one a day to maximise the audience they reach and how the engagement algorithms promote them.

Another benefit of this approach is that it allows me to post to social media retrospectively rather than interrupting my adventure. I'd rather enjoy leaping into the icy river and sort out the story-telling next week with a cup of tea. Once you forfeit the immediacy of 'now', I think you might as well tell the story thoroughly and schedule your posts to reach a wider audience.

Everything I post on Instagram automatically goes to Facebook, spreading the message more widely with no effort. You can also make those images show up properly on Twitter with a little tweak (search: 'IFTTT Tweet your Instagrams as native photos on Twitter'). Whilst there are good arguments for putting different content on different platforms (they have different demographics, for one thing), there's also a lot to be said for amplifying your message efficiently, without doing unnecessary extra work.

HOW DO I START A BLOG ABOUT MY OWN MICROADVENTURES? IT'S A MAZE OF INFORMATION ONLINE.

Don't overthink it. The main thing is just that you start. What is your priority: words, photos or video? If you like taking pics and jotting down a few thoughts, Instagram would do the job perfectly. If you like making films, then start uploading to YouTube. If you only want to write, Medium is super. If you're going to be an expert who answers questions, Quora might be your place. If you don't know exactly, begin your own website with Squarespace and start putting all your different work up there. Whichever social media angle you opt for, you definitely want to build up content on your own website.

What matters the most is getting out on those microadventures and turning your experiences into regular quality 'content'. Good luck.

CONNECTING

How can I improve my email newsletter?

What was the first social media platform you signed up for? MSN Messenger? Myspace? Friends Reunited? Facebook? Tumblr? Google+? Instagram? TikTok? Clubhouse?

The answer doesn't matter. What matters is realising that social media platforms come and go. The paragraph above will sound completely out of date in a few years.

Next question: When did you first use email? Have you read an email today? Email is unchanging, and it is everywhere. My hunch is that we will all still be using email when today's hottest social media platforms are but a nostalgic memory.

Therefore, if you are starting as a Working Adventurer, I would urge you to begin a newsletter immediately and start building an email list as well as growing an audience on whichever social media platforms appeal to you to focus on. Set up your own blog on your own website; a small corner of the internet that actually belongs to you, and will do so forever (for me, that is www.AlastairHumphreys. com). Gathering the email addresses of people interested in what you are doing is vital for anyone hoping to earn an income from their creative work. Be sure only to collect the email addresses of those who are happy for you to do so, of course. Make it easy for anyone to sign up for your newsletter on your website, through your social media bios and email footer. Mine are at www.AlastairHumphreys.

com/newsletters

For a long time, I cared only about how many subscribers had signed up to my list. These days I care far more about engagement levels (i.e. how interested an audience is, rather than merely how big it is.) Over 20 years, I had accumulated a list of more than 40,000 email addresses. Inevitably, a number of those became obsolete over time. So I began a pruning process, removing all the dead email addresses. Then I went further, emailing everyone to check whether they wanted to remain on my list and offering instant ways to unsubscribe if they did not. I even culled anyone who hadn't opened one of my newsletters in recent months! I was ruthless.

The result of all this was that my email list now stands at 18,000 readers. This is not as good for my ego as 40,000 was, and it will cost me money the next time a brand considers hiring me or paying for a mention in the newsletter. But it is more realistic, it's far more engaged (which is important for evading Spam filters), and it is much cheaper. It also has barely changed the numbers who actually open each newsletter. For the price of a vanity metric, I have improved my newsletter's deliverability and saved over £600 per year.

Think of this like a party. You can throw one of those parties posted on Facebook where masses of strangers turn up, eat all the snacks, wreck your house and then the police arrive and shut everything down. You can have a party where you invite everyone you've ever known (including a bunch of guests who don't even want to be there), and you never get to talk to your actual friends because you spend the whole night pushing through crowds of strangers. Or you can throw a party for a specific group of friends who are all on the same wavelength. Everyone has a brilliant time, and both you and they can't wait to do it all again soon. That is what you should aim for with your newsletter.

Like everything else in this book, I began small. I gathered email addresses from people who read my blog or came to my talks, copy/pasted them into the BCC section of an email and told them the news from my adventures. As the list grew, I moved on to Google Groups to keep people updated on my upcoming speaking events or books I had written. Over time I have moved through mailing options such as TinyLetter (really nice and simple), MailChimp (once my list got too big for TinyLetter), Sendy and MailWizz (once MailChimp got too expensive) and MailerLite, which I am currently happy with. As always, the platform you choose does not matter nearly so much as what you do with it.

One avenue I have not yet explored are subscription-based newsletters where readers pay to receive your content. They are becoming popular, and some writers are having success with it. Yet as a reader, I don't want to pay to receive email. I have enough books to read without paying for more emails. That perspective tempers my enthusiasm for trying this route as a writer. I am also wary of how many eyeballs I would lose by restricting access to the paying few. My approach is to try to grow a large, engaged audience through free email newsletters and hope readers will become motivated to buy one of my books or buy me a 'virtual coffee' through an online tip jar (www.ko-fi.com/al_humphreys) if they find my writing helpful.

There are many different ways to approach an email newsletter. Ask yourself these questions when trying to decide your own direction:

- Which newsletters do you enjoy receiving? Why do you like them?
- Which newsletters that you receive do not work well? Why not?
- How often do you like receiving newsletters? Daily? Weekly? Monthly? Only when they have something to sell you?
- What will be your aim when you send out a newsletter?
- What is your 'elevator pitch' that you will consider every time you write?
- What niche will you focus on?
- Who is your audience? Try to imagine your most committed reader when you write a newsletter and pitch it for them.
- How much good stuff do you have to share? How much time and effort are you willing to put into your newsletter?
- Are you looking to share curated content from other websites and blogs in your niche, or will you send out original content of your own? The latter option is better but more challenging, putting you in a better position to be an authority in your niche, whilst at the same time getting thousands of words written, which you can later convert into a book.

Sending newsletters is not as simple as emailing your granny to arrange a game of squash and then receiving her reply. Once you start emailing large numbers of folk, most of your messages do not even get opened. I am happy if 40% of my emails are opened, and 8% of readers click on a link. (The newsletter series that preceded this book, The Working Adventurer, has a 60% open rate which helped convince me that it was worth writing the book.) Some of the emails you send will be automatically, if erroneously, siphoned as Spam. Most are archived, deleted, or ignored by the recipients. Those who don't read your newsletters hurt your overall deliverability and cost you money, so it is important to be ruthless in removing deadwood.

You can take many actions to improve all these statistics, but (yet again) the best approach is to produce superb content over a long period. Make your newsletters mean something and fill them with meaty information that improves our days. None of us needs more boring emails in our lives. I will resist diving down into the nerdy rabbit holes of opening rates, optimal sending times, A/B testing and whitelisting, but once you get your newsletter established, I would urge you to read up on those.

How you create your newsletter is up to you. Do you want to tell stories? To be a useful expert? To grow your audience? Or simply to sell stuff? Whatever you settle on, you should be focused. Once you are clear about your tone and message, repeat, repeat, repeat it. I have spent so many years writing blog posts about 'how to sleep on a hill' and sending out links in newsletters about 'people who are living adventurously, why don't you try that too?' Yet, the numbers of subscribers who are interested in that only continues to grow.

I try to keep my newsletters personal as though it is an email from a friend rather than a corporation. I ask readers to reply to me with their thoughts. I ask questions about how I can make my newsletters more beneficial for them. What do you want? How often do you want it? Over time, the content of my newsletter has evolved. I still include news of what I have been up to, but my focus is much more on providing a curated collection of nuggets that interest me. I do this because I don't have so many big adventures to talk about and because I don't have enough time to write regular essays for a newsletter.

Many people who write about growing email lists advise that you should have something to give away. 'Sign up for my newsletter and receive a free ebook about how to get a six-pack in six weeks.' (Note: I have *never* signed up for that newsletter…) It is an effective way to gather email addresses and worth trying if you have suitable materials to give away. But the cheap immediacy of it makes me doubt how engaged or interested those new sign-ups will be in the long run.

A sure-fire way for your newsletter to be ignored or siphoned into Spam is if it is very sporadic. It is only marginally better than sending nothing to belong to the newsletter brigade of, 'Sorry I haven't been in touch for a year, but I've just published a book, and you can buy it now.'

You will have much more long-term success if your newsletters are regular (not the same as frequent), and they serve a purpose for your reader. That could be to entertain them, to keep them abreast of the genre you're an expert in, or to help them and teach them. I quickly tire of the 'me, me, me' newsletters, which read like the old 'boast in the post' letters from distant relatives sent in Christmas cards. Of course, you are trying to get something out of your newsletters, but it's a good habit to think of what you can give first and foremost. Give, give, give useful content so that when you then ask your readers for something, you have enough goodwill capital in the bank so that they are more likely to think, 'Oh, go on then.'

When you *do* ask your readers for something, don't bury it in embarrassment at the bottom of the email. Digital attentions are very fleeting, so you have to make your call to action clear, immediate and specific.

For example,

- I'd love you to buy a copy of my new book. You can order it <u>here</u> in the UK and <u>here</u> in every other country, with free worldwide shipping. Thank you.

Or,

- Getting books reviewed on Amazon makes a huge difference to independent authors like me. If you have read my book, could I please ask you to take 30 seconds and leave your honest opinion on it <u>here</u> or post a photo of the cover on your social media? Thank you.

One subject which has got me very excited recently is the world of automated email sequences. These are a fabulous subject to bring up in conversation in the pub if it's feeling a bit crowded and you'd like to clear some space around you. They are nerdy, yes, but they are both efficient and a good way for telling stories – two traits I hold dear as a Working Adventurer who would rather be out on my bike than setting up newsletters.

You will have experienced automated email sequences even if you don't realise it. You sign up for a newsletter and then receive a series of emails building on the subject over the coming days or weeks. Whilst I could spend time each week writing an email series about 'How to plan an adventure', I would much rather write it all in one go, automate it and then have a cup of tea whilst you enjoy the writing over several weeks.

Two of my newsletters (The Doorstep Mile and The Working Adventurer) work in precisely this way. I will use The Doorstep Mile as an example. I had the idea to write a series of free articles about dreaming big, overcoming the mental and practical barriers in our lives, and starting small in the direction we want to go. In the past, I would have written this as a blog series or a book. Instead, I set it up as a newsletter.

When somebody subscribes, they receive the first email introducing the subject. About a week later, they get the second email, and so on. The newsletter provides a constant drip of helpful content for an interested reader without me having to do anything more than the initial work of setting everything up. Such newsletters are an ideal format for growing your 1000 True Fans, particularly if you include an occasional call to action asking the reader to share it with anyone they know who might be interested.

I have written my last two books via automated email newsletters. Writing a scheduled sequence of posts forced me to knuckle down and get the words written. The feedback from readers helped me edit and improve what I had written. Then when all the articles were finished I could tweak and polish them into book chapters. I already knew I had a loyal audience who enjoyed what I had been writing about and might help me evangelise about the book. From my own experience as a reader, I also know that if I really enjoy a dozen of someone's blog posts on a topic, then I would want to own and read their book of all those compiled blog posts, even if I could seek out most of the material as individual blog posts online.

Bear in mind that you can't please all the people all of the time. Some readers will unsubscribe every time you send a newsletter. That is normal and perfectly fine. A few might also get very angry with you when receiving a newsletter they asked to receive. This is less normal, and you can choose whether to be upset or amused by these messages. I enjoy using a few angry responses as the customer endorsements on my website for trying to persuade new readers to subscribe:

- 'Prat!!! Do you really think people have time to read such crap? God knows who you could motivate having read that. Unsubscribed.'
- 'unsubscribing. you're rather a wordy bastard and all of them dull. cheers.'
- 'I've tried several times to unsubscribe from your horrendously sh*te, pish, crappy, useless and infuriating emails. They keep coming. Please can you **** off and leave me alone you absolute pr***.' [Asterisks placed by me, not my cheerful correspondent.]

This despite all my newsletters having a single-click, obvious Unsubscribe button...

WHAT BOOKS HAVE MOST INFLUENCED YOUR LIFE?

I have given many copies of *As I Walked Out One Midsummer Morning* as gifts, initially because I loved it as a travel story and latterly since I used it as the inspiration for my own busking adventure in Spain.

I used to give away copies of *It's Not About the Bike* by Lance Armstrong. It was so inspiring to me during the years I was cycling around the world and one of my strongest influences. I was gutted when it turned out to be not so much about the bike as the drugs.

Other books that have disproportionally influenced my life include:

- *Living Dangerously* was the first adventure book that captured my soul and made me realise that it was possible to live an unconventional, challenging life. Until I read that book by Ranulph Fiennes, every single figure in my life had been directing me (in a well-meaning way) down the usual route of school, university, job, pension, death.
- *The Quiet Soldier* is a book I read many times when I was young and learning to set high, self-motivated goals. In the end, I preferred to find my adventure in a world away from guns.
- *Man's Search for Meaning* by Viktor Frankl is a surprisingly upbeat read about life in a Nazi concentration camp. 'The one thing you can't take away from me is the way I choose to respond to what you do to me. The last of one's freedoms is to choose one's attitude in any given circumstance.'

How do you start a podcast?

In the summer of 2019, I cycled around Yorkshire interviewing adventurous people. These conversations became my first podcast, though I had never held a microphone up to someone and interviewed them like this before. The Living Adventurously podcast reached #15 in the UK chart for all podcasts (albeit very briefly), was showcased on Apple's New & Noteworthy page and had 300,000 downloads in its first year. It did far better than I could have imagined.

Yet, I only decided to record a podcast a few days before my ride began. I had planned to conduct the interviews for a book I hoped to write. But as I walked out of my shed one morning, I was halted in my tracks by a sudden epiphany: 'I should do a podcast on this trip!'

And so began a frenzy of Googling and last-minute shopping, culminating in me recording my first-ever podcast interview on the first-ever occasion I used my new equipment. This is not a technique to be recommended.

Podcasting has been a delightful experience. It is so much quicker than writing a book, less faff than editing a video and much simpler and cheaper. The best bit is that asking someone interesting if you can 'interview them for a podcast' is less cringey and more likely to succeed than asking, 'can we hang out together because I think you are fascinating?'

The simplest way to start a podcast is by recording the audio on your phone. I considered doing it that way myself to save weight on my ride. I would urge you to at least invest in a microphone for your phone, perhaps one from Rode or Sennheiser. Duff-sounding audio will deter even your keenest listeners. Once you have recorded a conversation, the easiest way to publish it is via the Anchor app, 'an all-in-one platform where you can create, distribute and monetise your podcast from any device, for free.' It is incredibly easy to enter the world of podcasting. The barriers are so low.

I decided to skip the test-it-out-cheaply approach to podcasts and went for the other sensible option: spend enough money upfront to coerce you into action and commitment. I did this because there was not enough time before my trip began to experiment and because I'm generally impatient.

I kept things simple. I decided to just copy the gear Tim Ferriss uses in his wildly successful podcast. If it is good enough for millions of listeners, it would be good enough for me. Ten minutes of Googling, ten minutes of online shopping, and a shiny selection of gear was winging its way to me. Having now tested the equipment in 65 interviews, I can belatedly vouch for and recommend all my choices.

- Zoom H6 Recorder. Online nerds spend a lot of time arguing between the H6 and the H4. I didn't get involved in that. All I know is that the model I plumped for works a treat. The key thing that a recorder like this does, which your phone cannot do, is record up to six tracks separately (i.e. my microphone and your microphone generate different tracks). This is useful if you have to do any tricky editing, such as if you have the annoying habit of saying 'uh-huh' throughout your guest's answer or if they speak more softly than you.
- Two Shure SM58 microphones and 6-foot XLR cables. On top of my mics are 'dead kittens', the fluffy windstopper thingies that are essential if you are going to record outside. Make sure both you and your guest know how to hold a microphone correctly. I recommend keeping it fixed to your chin, ensuring an even level of audio recording at all times. The long cables allow you and your guest to sit a comfortable distance apart from each other.
- Wired headphones to monitor audio levels during conversations. Foolishly, it took me a few interviews to realise how important constant monitoring of the levels is. I settled on a system of having one earphone in place to monitor the levels and the other out to engage more completely with the person I was interviewing. I found it tiring to keep an eye on the levels, the guest and my sheet of questions all whilst chatting away.
- 64GB SD storage card. This is far more storage than you need for an audio recorder, but you do not want to run out of space mid-interview.
- Lots of AA batteries for the recorder. You do not want to run out of batteries mid-interview.
- My phone with the Otter app installed to record the conversation. This recording acted as a backup if something went wrong with the

main recorder and produced AI transcripts that saved a lot of time later on.

- My daughter's floral lunch box to carry it all in.

Whilst buying shiny kit is the fun part of your podcasting debut, a far more useful phase is figuring out what you will speak about. Will you go for an engaging monologue about something you are an expert at, like Hardcore History, tell a long story like Serial, chat with your mates like No Such Thing as a Fish or interview different guests like How I Built This? Your podcast can be as short or as long as you like. Personally, I enjoy listening to episodes that are up to one hour long, so that was the length I settled on. It doesn't matter what you do, so long as you say something interesting. If you don't, then you do not pass Go, do not collect £200 and do not have much chance of putting together a successful podcast.

Before each interview, I spent hours learning about each guest. I have been interviewed on many podcasts and find it tedious when the host has done zero homework and asks predictable, formulaic questions. I didn't want to inflict that on my guests. The downside of having a long list of prepared questions was that it was hard to decide, mid-conversation, whether to meander off on detours or keep to the structure. A bit of both is probably the ideal answer.

Dare yourself to remain silent when your guest seems to have finished answering a profound question. That is when the good stuff often comes out if you allow it to. We have two ears and one mouth for a reason. Listen more than you speak. I do not like podcasts when the interviewer seizes every opportunity to talk about themselves, asks annoyingly long questions or makes statements rather than asking questions. Yet these tics might be exactly what you want in your podcast. The beauty of podcasts is that you can do it however you like, far more so than in virtually any other form of published medium. Just be sure to think carefully and consider each aspect and detail deliberately.

An excellent way to do this is to listen to lots of podcasts before recording your own. Copy the parts you like, reject the bits you don't. For me, that meant not interviewing the same group of people I hear on every adventure podcast, and it meant not having an advert in the middle of an episode, regardless of how much sponsors want one.

Once you have finished recording and backed up your SD card, the next step is to get the conversation out into the world. For reasons of laziness and efficiency, I decided in advance that I would not edit my interviews beyond topping and tailing the beginning and end. I did reassure my guests that I could edit out anything they were uncomfortable with. This never happened, but it felt like the right thing to do as well as a way to put them at ease. If you go down the no-edit route, you need to be on the ball during the interview to keep the pace, direction and duration of the conversation under control.

There are software programmes that remove the hisses and peaks that sound jarring and distracting. For reasons of laziness and efficiency, I paid someone to do this, polishing the audio, splicing on my introduction and exporting the files into the optimum format to go online.

The part that confused me the most before launching a podcast was how to get it onto all the different podcast apps. It is actually straightforward. The company you choose to host your podcast with stores the files and zaps them magically out on your behalf to Apple, Spotify and all the other apps. How much you pay the host depends upon how many listeners you end up with. There are several major hosting companies, but they all seem to do pretty much the same thing. For reasons of laziness and efficiency once again, I just plumped for the recommendation of a podcaster I trusted and signed up with Transistor. It is intuitive, works perfectly and has good analytics and customer support.

Once you have signed up with a hosting company, you upload the material for each episode: the audio file, cover art and introductory text. You do a chunk of clicking here and there to get it all linked up to the various podcast apps, but even a dimwit like me did it quickly enough.

You don't have to go live immediately upon loading an episode, and I urge you not to. Give yourself plenty of time before launch day. It takes up to two weeks for a show to be listed on the Apple podcast site, so be sure to submit a teaser episode to get in the pipeline before your planned launch. Apple is the biggest podcast provider, so it would be foolish to launch before everything is in their system. The most popular apps for listening to my podcast are Apple Podcasts then Spotify. Significantly lower come Castbox, Podcast Addict and

Overcast. Finally, there is a long tail of all sorts of other apps that my podcast gets automatically listed on.

Once you have recorded some magnificent content and uploaded it all, you need to give some thought to launch day. It works well to launch with a few episodes simultaneously. I put out five episodes, allowing early adopters an early binge and an easy boost up the rankings. From then on, I released a new episode at 5 am every Tuesday, without fail, for over a year.

As with publishing a book, the day you launch your podcast is not the end of the hard work. You need to make an effort to find and grow an audience for your new baby. Getting a spike of early listens helps trick the internet algorithms into thinking that you are amazing, just like when you publish a book. It is a powerful way to get your podcast heard by a new audience who might be interested in what you have done. You'll need to employ all the usual marketing tactics to secure an early spike of listens – social media, newsletters, asking for reviews etc. Push hard (to the cusp of annoying your audience) to get people to listen to your podcast in Hour 1, Day 1 and Week 1. Because I had high hopes for my podcast, I even WhatsApped every person in my phone, asking them to listen. I have never done that before.

If all goes well and you get enough listeners, you have a chance of being listed on the Apple New & Noteworthy chart which has a vast audience. However, as always, I issue a cautionary caveat that whilst I did see a sizeable early spike of new listeners, virtually all of them disappeared after a week or so. Better, as always in the life of the Working Adventurer, to build slow, steady, loyal audiences through positive reviews and word of mouth.

Running a podcast involves time, equipment and hosting costs. You are, hopefully, producing a quality product that will add value to lives and therefore can justly be monetised. But I initially couldn't be bothered to find a sponsor for my podcast. I wanted to be 'pure', to 'not sell out' and stuff like that. Then a wise friend sat me down and said politely, 'You're an idiot.'

So I sent some episodes to various companies, asking if they would like to sponsor the show. It is tough to sell an unknown entity like a new podcast before it has launched. All I could say was, 'I have no idea how many people will listen. X people follow me on other platforms, but this podcast is brand new. It could be 10, it could be 10 million. Your guess is as good as mine! Fancy taking a punt?'

At last, komoot decided to give it a go and sponsor the podcast's first series. I was delighted: komoot is a fantastic brand, perfectly aligned with what I do. We tussled amicably about the length of the advert and whether they could have their advert mid-episode (nope). My agent and komoot locked themselves in a dark room to talk numbers. Then komoot licked their finger, squinted into the wind and gave me a low five-figure sum to sponsor Series 1, all 42 episodes of it.

I believe that the listening stats from even the first few months meant that komoot got a good deal in terms of a highly targeted listener demographic receiving a weekly drip-drip of name-recognition advertising. Plus, the podcast won't go away, so they will benefit from those ads for years to come (and this plug in my book). I am enormously grateful to komoot for taking a punt on my debut podcast. I hope that, over time, enough people listen to the accumulation of episodes for them to feel that they got a decent return on their money.

Unfortunately, komoot decided not to sponsor the second series of the podcast. That's fine, of course. Marketing plans change all the time, plus it is difficult to put a tangible, precise number on what counts as 'value for money' for a podcast. The KPIs – Key Performance Indicators – are hazy and moveable, and perhaps komoot measure podcast success in a different way to me.

All of which is a long way of saying that it is difficult to find a sponsor for a brand-new podcast. I would recommend you treat any funds you do secure as a bonus rather than a prerequisite for beginning. It costs me £350 a year to host my podcast. If you start out with a small audience then you won't be charged anything. An average of 4000 people listen to each episode within the first 90 days, in over 100 countries, with over 300,000 listens in the first year. The wider rewards of my podcast have been reaching a different audience, learning from those I met along the way, making new friends and having a good time.

I was surprised by the power a microphone gives you. Shove a microphone under someone's nose, and they seem duty-bound to provide honest and thoughtful answers to whatever topic tickles your curiosity. All these fascinating folk (most of whom I had never met before) welcomed me generously and patiently and indulged me with my quirky deck of question cards. The whole experience was a delightful privilege.

I have enjoyed everything about diving into the world of podcasting, and its impact (judging from email feedback) has been more profound than I imagined. If you are tempted to start a podcast, I would say try it. It is so quick, cheap and easy that it is worth recording a handful of episodes and then deciding if you want to continue beyond that. I have been surprised by how many people I meet have still never listened to a podcast, nor even quite understand what they are. Popular though it is, podcasting is by no means a saturated market, and you are not too late to join in. Go on: give your podcast idea a try.

WHAT ARE YOUR FAVOURITE PODCASTS?

Desert Island Discs, In Our Time, Armchair Expert, That Peter Crouch Podcast, Renegades, Tim Ferriss, 99% Invisible, Cal Fussman, Cal Newport, Creative Rebels, The Adventure Podcast, Folk on Foot, Soul Music, Rule of Three, Hurry Slowly, Frank Skinner's Poetry, Saving Apollo 13 and, of course, Living Adventurously.

Do you recommend filming adventures or does it take the joy out of it?

Some adventurers have no interest in the story-telling aspect of adventures. We don't know who they are because they do their trips merely for their own satisfaction and don't tell us about them. I understand and occasionally envy this approach.

But I have always enjoyed sharing my journeys. Whilst the trip is in progress I like pondering how I might communicate what I am experiencing. I began this daydreaming process whilst cycling round the world, imagining how I might try to turn the experience into a book. It whiled away many a happy mile.

Later, walking across India, I focused on trying to tell the story through photography. It helped me be more observant and led to a richer journey than if I had simply trudged through every day with my head down.

With the arrival of SLR cameras that could also record HD video, I decided to learn a new skill. I saw an opportunity to get ahead of the curve and be in the vanguard of a niche, filming adventures with an emphasis on the aesthetic beauty of the landscapes. I crossed Iceland to teach myself how to wield my new video camera. On top of the photography, I loved the daily technical conundrums wrapped up with all the hiking, camping and packrafting.

I have since spent many hours of my life setting up a tripod, walking a long way past the camera (or cycling, running, canoeing or swimming) then trudging all the way back again to collect the gear! Endless walk-bys and repeating activities over and over when all you want to do is sleep is the reality of self-filmed expeditions.

I know my ISO from my f-stops now, but an ISO does not a story make and the process of learning how to edit and produce a narrative out of all the raw footage is a tremendously involved art. I have relished devoting colossal amounts of time and brainpower to learning some of the skills, though I still only consider myself an enthusiastic amateur. Making films, even tiny ones for YouTube like I do, demands so much time and effort.

Here are a few issues to consider before deciding whether you want to film an adventure or if you should stick to writing, photography or just enjoying the peace and quiet of the journey itself.

What do you want to get out of filming? A few snippets for your sponsors or to use in presentations, a short souvenir film, an expedition distilled down to a couple of minutes to hoover up eyeballs on YouTube, or a much longer documentary for film festivals or Netflix? What style of film are you interested in? Beautiful and serene, Krazy and Xtreme, informative, or heart-wrenching? You need to be very clear about all this before you begin.

Filming an expedition properly will cost a lot of money and it is unlikely that you will make a profit. Editing the film may well entail more hours of work than the trip itself. Are you up for the long haul? What rewards are you after? What would you consider success to look like?

Are all your team members agreed on how extensively you are going to film? If not, you run the risk of filming half-heartedly whilst still annoying the guy who wants to be covering more miles each day. The quality of story-telling always sinks to the level of the least enthusiastic team member.

Are you able to plan your story in advance? The more that you can plan the film, the better. In reality, of course, the joy of adventure is not knowing what is going to happen next. This inevitably leads to endless anxious conversations every time the key point of your film is suddenly (and repeatedly) rendered obsolete by changing circumstances. I relish this back and forth which continues long after the adventure into the pubs and edit-suites of the following months.

Dreams of film-making quickly morph into coveting expensive cameras and lenses. But the phone in your pocket is perfectly capable of capturing a Netflix blockbuster, so long as you can find the right story for it. Before investing in expensive camera equipment I would concentrate on buying a tripod, a microphone and capturing the story thoughtfully. Good audio is at least as important as good video and much cheaper.

When you are on your trip you will need to be prepared to film even when you do not want to film. *Especially* when you don't want to film. You must record the stuff you can't be bothered to record. Tents blowing away, misery in the rain, near-death disasters: this is what everyone really wants to watch.

Filming an adventure takes so much longer than photographing one and involves lugging a lot more heavy gear around. It invades your experience more than writing or giving talks and costs much more too. It completely changes the feeling of being away in the wilderness or having conversations with people you meet along the way. On the plus side, producing films is intellectually rewarding and addictive. I love the entire process.

YOU MUST HAVE TAKEN THOUSANDS OF PHOTOGRAPHS ON YOUR ADVENTURES. IS IT POSSIBLE TO BOIL THIS DOWN TO ONE PARTICULAR PICTURE THAT INVOKES THE MOST POWERFUL MEMORIES AND FEELINGS?

I could happily pore over old photographs for hours of nostalgia to answer this question, or I could pick the instant answer that my gut suggests. My choice is apt because it is a photo I love, but it is also a self-timer photo, posed and taken in the knowledge that it would be helpful for telling the story later. Adventurer meets Working Adventurer...

In the picture I'm thinking of, I am sitting on top of sand dunes in front of a sea full of crashing waves. I'm all alone. The sun is warm and low as sunset approaches. I will sleep on this beach tonight. Alongside me is my bike, laden with panniers and camping gear. I am holding a bottle of champagne in both hands, a gift from a family of strangers who became friends. I look tired, happy, perhaps a little disbelieving. My hair is long and curly, bleached golden by a year of African sunshine. The photograph is taken at Cape Point in South Africa. I am celebrating and relaxing after cycling from England to the foot of Africa. I am alone but happy, 25 years old and so many adventures still to come. That photograph sums up much of what I have loved about my years of adventure. You can see it at www.bit.ly/ChampagnePhoto

GENERAL QUESTIONS

How do you become an adventurer?

If you're not in it for the money, you become an adventurer by lacing up your boots and going out on adventures. Simple as that.

If you want to be a Working Adventurer and earn a living, you begin by lacing up your boots and heading out. The adventures you choose need to have something about them that will be interesting to other people. The next step is to tell your stories or use your talents in ways that someone will pay for. Whether that is through photography, writing, speaking, guiding, teaching, or social influencing will depend upon the skills you have and what direction you want to go.

In the meantime, you must also have a plan for earning money until enough comes in from your adventures, whilst still allowing enough time to begin growing an audience. Finally, lob in a large dollop of self-promotion, patience and perseverance, and you're away.

Think about what your motives are for choosing this direction. If you are motivated by money, there are better career options to choose from. An alternative to becoming a Working Adventurer is to be somebody who goes on adventures when they are not at work.

Someone with a proper job and a hobby, in other words.

Consider also the fairly reliable correlation that wealthier adventurers generally live less adventurously than dirtbags who live out of vans but go climbing every day.

It is also important to acknowledge that lingering beneath these pages are the advantages I have gained from being well-educated. If things don't work out as a Working Adventurer, I can quickly find other work. That is an important safety net to have. Being literate and relatively eloquent has made my creative life easier. For the physical adventures that are the basis of my stories, things have run more smoothly for me by being able-bodied, white and male, as they are for pretty much everything in life. As for my incredible good looks, I can only say that they account for my delightful modesty.

It will probably take years before you write an excellent book, get involved with prestigious projects, or earn much more than a living wage. You will need to work long hours. You'll need self-discipline and to manage your time well, just like anyone running their own small business. You must enjoy the process and all the stages of the journey.

What you do not need when you begin is any firm idea about where your fledgling career will go. The path will twist and turn on your long apprenticeship. You must be willing to accept that success will not happen instantly. You need to be in it for the long run. Too many people set the cart before the horse, seeking the honour and recognition but without first completing the hazardous journey on low wages in the bitter cold through long hours of complete darkness.

'Ready, fire, aim' is an excellent attitude for just getting started, launching in and figuring stuff out as you go. It's the way most adventurers operate, and it keeps life interesting, so long as you accept that it is likely to take a long time before you hit whatever target it is that you're aiming at.

There is a lot of dubious 'quit your job to follow your dreams' advice out there. This is marvellous if you're minted but daft for everyone else. If you want to do change direction and do something different with your working life, my advice is to start small. Fill your weekends and spare time with what you love whilst still plugging away at the day job. Become competent at your passion and build your new skills, both in the thing itself and in the story-telling or practical side of it that might give you a route to earning money. Photography, writing, speaking, film-making, guiding – whatever it is, you need to get good at something beyond the journey itself if you are going to make adventure pay.

Work like mad juggling all the different balls in your life. When it gets too much, consider trading a day of your working week for a day of your passion. Continue the process, little by little, until one day you realise you are earning enough from your adventures to make a fist of it. Only then would I urge you to take the leap and quit your everyday life for the new one. Then, work, work, work and one day you might become an overnight success (or at least get paid to do what you love, which is even better.)

WHAT IS HARDER TO BEAR: HOT AND DRY OR COLD AND WET?
Cold and wet, by far.

When did you know you wanted to devote your life to being a Working Adventurer?

I began daydreaming of life as an adventurer in my first year at university to get me through boring lectures and working long hours in the pub to save travel money. It was nothing more than that, though: a dusty daydream in the recesses of my mind. I didn't imagine that I would actually be able to get by without having a 'proper' job. My early adventures were not only precious experiences in themselves, but they also paved the way to becoming a Working Adventurer through a gradual sequence of stages towards acceptance and ownership. First, I had to define the direction I wanted to go and believe it myself. Then I had to dare to describe myself that way online and finally say it to real people face-to-face. I still never manage to do this without air quotes, deprecation and explanations. 'Adventurer' is a ridiculous job description for a middle-aged bloke.

When someone asks me what my job is, I usually say that I am a writer, despite that not making up a majority of my income (*yet*, he adds, in hope). Writing does occupy a majority of my working time though, so perhaps that *is* what I am? After all, we are what we repeatedly do.

At other times, when I can't be bothered with the inevitable conversation that follows from saying I am an adventurer or a writer, I say I am a teacher. I was a teacher, once upon a time, after all. And if I'm in one of those dangerous situations for introverts where you can't escape your inquisitor and the horrors of small talk, I shut the conversation down fast by saying that I'm an accountant (experience has shown me that this leads to very few follow-up questions) and then burying my nose in a book.

Upon returning from cycling around the world, the financial urgency of paying rent thrust me immediately into a semblance of the writing and speaking work that I still do today. I did not consider that it would become a permanent way of life. I was only getting my feet back on the ground after four years alone in strange corners of the world. I was also busy applying for 'real' jobs at the same time: the Army, the fire brigade, a travel agency, a charity, schools. The variety of these shows that I was not pursuing a clear vocation yet.

[A quick pause for my favourite interview recollection...
Interviewer: 'So, why do you want this job?'
Me: 'Well, I'm not sure if I do want it, to be honest. I'd also really like to be a fireman.'
Interviewer: 'I think we'll just end the interview now.'
Then the man kindly gave me about 15 minutes of interview technique advice!
Next interview I attended:
Interviewer: 'So, why do you want this job?'
Me: 'I've always wanted this job because...'
And I got the job.]

Fast forward through various bits and bobs, and I became a full-time teacher at a school in London. I enjoyed it, but I was also busily writing a book and hustling for paid magazine articles and talks around the margins of my days and in my spare time. The idea of becoming a Working Adventurer was beginning to take shape. The independence appealed. Being my own boss would allow me to be flexible with my time, earn money from my hobbies and not have to wear a suit.

At some point in that school year, it dawned on me that I was 30 years old. It was perfectly plausible that I could now remain teaching in that school for as long as the entire span of life I had already lived! The prospect appalled me. I also knew that I could be a good teacher aged 40 or 50 or 60. But if I still wanted to pursue hard expeditions, which I did, then I ought to get on with it while I still had gas in the tank and few constraints in my life. I told the headteacher that I wanted to leave.

'Oh! Where are you going?'
'South Pole.'
'St. Paul's? Lovely school!'

Cue the delightful terror of waking up on Monday morning with nowhere to go, no suit to wear, nobody to answer to and no money coming my way.

159

From that first day of self-employment, I knew that if I was to reconcile this reckless career decision with my conventional, sensible work ethic, then I faced a hard, scrabbling climb to establish myself and make a go of it. I was never under any illusion that I was plumping for an option that was less work. Yet, equally, I have never since been under any illusion at how lucky I am to have found work that is enjoyable, unshackled, mentally and physically stretching, carefree, vaguely useful and sufficiently remunerative.

IF YOU COULD HAVE BEEN PART OF ONE OF HISTORY'S GREAT EXPEDITIONS, WHICH ONE WOULD YOU HAVE CHOSEN?

Even though they all died (spoiler alert), I have always had great admiration for the spirit, kindness and friendship inside Captain Scott's tent on his doomed final journey. I wish I could have been there to whisper a couple of suggestions that would have saved their lives with the clarity of hindsight.

I would love to have tagged along with Mallory and Irvine to see if they made it to Everest's summit way back in 1924. Although, given that they both died (spoiler alert) and were dressed like a pair of geography teachers in woolly jumpers and tweed, I'm not sure I would actually have wanted to be tied in on their rope.

Since reading *Over the Edge of the World*, I have been intrigued about dropping off the edge of the map with Magellan and his crew. Imagine setting off to sail the Pacific with no idea of how big it was or what land you would stumble upon next!

But, without doubt, my dream would be to have stowed away in the Lunar Module *Eagle* with Armstrong and Aldrin and landed on the moon. What an astonishing adventure.

Who do you envy in the adventure world?

While I was writing this chapter, someone asked me which characteristic of admiration, envy, or resentment might my younger self apply to my current self? I think it would be a mixture of all three. Admiration that I have managed some feats that the younger me was ambitious to do. Envy that I receive sponsored bikes and outdoor gear. And resentment that I get them despite doing far less actual adventuring than I did 20 years ago.

I am not the only Working Adventurer out there. If you rummage online, you'll find plenty of us. We don't work together or have a union that represents us. But many of my good friends are adventurers. Some of my favourite evenings are when adventurers gather in a pub after an event. Away from our public faces and anecdotes, we relax, laugh a lot, talk nonsense and share the unspoken realities of our lives.

I don't consider the world of adventure to be a zero-sum world where I must lose if you win, so I do not feel in competition with other Working Adventurers. This is perhaps easier for me than others because I'm not in the business of first, fastest or furthest.

Locked away in my shed, I'm generally free from the politics, hierarchy and gossip that can generate resentment in working life. I confess I have not been immune to it in the past, though I'm mellower and less competitive these days. I am also well aware that I hold more than my fair share of 'privileged life' cards.

There is an important distinction between the people I admire and those I envy. I love hearing about journeys that clearly come from the heart, where the person doing it would be fully engrossed in the challenge even if nobody else ever heard about it. For that reason, I'm turned off by trips that seem to be primarily about bagging a world record. Doing something you have never done, to the best of your ability, is what matters to me. If that leads to a world record, then congratulations. But picking an adventure just so that it can become something to show off about leaves me cold.

I look up to those who are better than me at what they do and feel only positive towards them. They provide me with joy, insight and ideas. They light the way for me to follow meekly but contentedly behind, motivating me to aspire and improve. I work hard to reach their levels. I do not resent them. Instead, I learn from them. If someone tackles an epic journey, writes a fabulous book, or creates a glorious film, I hold my hands up and applaud.

I admire anyone who strives for absolute excellence in one tiny niche of adventure. I've never had the drive or sticking power to chase those marginal gains, so I respect seeing accomplishments that are far beyond my mental resolve or my physical capabilities.

Specific to my role as a Working Adventurer, here are a few folk who are exceptionally good at the things that I do:

- Alex Honnold's simple, focused, undistracted lifestyle: 'I like climbing. Therefore I will do it a lot and do it well.'
- Ranulph Fiennes and Borge Ousland's expedition pedigree.
- Kate Harris and Robert Macfarlane's writing.
- Temujin Doran and Renan Ozturk's film-making. [Watch the film Mountain for a gorgeous partnering of Ozturk and Macfarlane's skills.]
- Ben Saunders' success in the public speaking world.
- Sarah Outen's commitment to doing one thing well – one whopping expedition, then a labour of love to get the film of the trip just the way she wanted it.
- Jimmy Chin, Chris Burkard and Martin Hartley's photography.
- Tim Ferriss' success at earning a living from doing what he enjoys and hanging out with interesting podcast guests.
- Maria Popova's substantial, brilliantly networked, thoughtful website.
- Seth Godin's persistent creation of helpful, positive content.
- Paul Jarvis' 'company of one' ethos.

We live in an era where social media magnifies and festers envy in all directions. Chasing social media 'likes' is to build a fool's castle on foundations of sand. But, at the same time, growing a decent-sized social media audience was vital to me becoming a viable Working Adventurer. Therefore I have, at times, envied people with large online reaches. There are several reasons why someone might have a bigger audience than me: bigger biceps or boobs annoys me, but bigger adventures or better stories inspire me.

I have often felt envious of adventurers who have won Travel Writing awards, won the Banff Film Festival, or had a film shown at the Kendal Mountain Film Festival. I have never managed any of these. The sensible response to my annual disappointments should be to work harder and improve. Don't allow a judging panel's opinion to be my measure of self-worth. But my envious side can sometimes stamp its feet and shout that it's not fair. They've got better marketing teams. They've got ghostwriters or camera crews. The judges don't like me!

Writing this made me feel like a shrivelled, shrewish sourpuss. So I paused for a few minutes to counterpoint it by considering all that I *do* have and *am* grateful for. That was a much more fruitful exercise. (Such reminders are why I like the Dollar Street website.) I have cheered up again now.

Another aspect to the question of envy relates to lifestyles in general, away from the world of Working Adventurers. I envy those who are not restless and feel content, regardless of their walk of life. I envy those who are fulfilling their potential, are happy doing so and are making the world a better place.

I am also envious if you live in the mountains / by the sea / in a village with a great café / in a van / in California / the Pyrenees / Reykjavik and on and on and on…

DO YOU EVER DO FRIENDLY CHALLENGES WITH OTHER ADVENTURERS?

No, because I am better than all of them at everything. And I'm not competitive at all…

How strong is your need for recognition?

Ooh, this is a good question to get me squirming in the therapist's chair. My need for recognition is strong, although greatly diminished these days. I deplore in myself the desire to win the praise of others, but acknowledging that motivator has been a helpful step towards growing up.

I definitely wanted to cycle around the world to garner some recognition and attention. (Polar explorer Robert Swann admitted that one of his motives was 'to impress girls at parties'.) I had felt ordinary and under-rated all my life. I wanted to differentiate myself from other people and show the world and myself that I could accomplish something substantial.

Later, when I began posting articles and films online, I used to pay close attention to how many comments and views they generated. Eventually, I had to ban myself from studying Google Analytics for my website or my Amazon sales rank position as I got a bit addicted to those metrics. I reasoned that if I just focused on producing good stuff, everything else would work out OK.

I used to direct my professional envy towards those drawing more recognition than me, suggesting a craving for the spotlight. Nowadays, however, I don't really care about recognition at all. I do the projects I want to do because they interest me. If I am happy with a book I've written, that feels enough, even if hardly anyone reads it. I am uncertain whether this comes from a mellowing of age or because I have gained sufficient of an audience so that a few folk notice whatever I do, and that small dose of attention is enough to keep my vanity satisfied.

HAVE YOU EVER BEEN RECOGNISED ON THE STREETS?

Years ago, I was going through a phase of associating success as a Working Adventurer with fame. I spent a day filming something with Ben Fogle and was struck by everyone recognising him, everyone turning to look as we passed, everyone wanting to say hello to him. I realised then that I had zero desire to be famous.

I have only been recognised a few times, and I find it extremely embarrassing. The first time it happened, I was on a busy rush-hour train into London. The carriage was crowded but self-consciously silent, as commuter trains tend to be. A man got onto the train and squeezed onto the seat opposite me. He peered at me and then said, 'Oh my God! Are you Alastair Humphreys?'

All eyes in the carriage swivelled our way. Panicked, I blurted out the first thing that came into my head. 'No mate, not me. Sorry.'

I promptly felt like a total doofus. But I then couldn't think of a way to back out of what I had done. So we sat opposite each other in silence for about 30 minutes until the train arrived in London, with the man clearly knowing that I had just denied that I was me, and me feeling extremely awkward!

How do you keep your ego in check?

I am not sure what prompted someone to ask this question. I'd prefer not to know, perhaps. Yet, for all my many faults, I'm proud to say that I don't think ego is one of them. I deserve a medal for my modesty. I know I do many things better than many people. I also know that someone else does every aspect of what I do better than me. I feel comfortable with accepting my place in the hierarchy of a meritocratic world.

Similarly, I don't really worry about whether an adventure I do is 'publishable' or will impress the public. If I want to do the trip, I do it. If I want to document it, I do that. The choice as to whether something ought to become a Tweet, a blog post or a book depends entirely on my appetite for the work required. Plenty of adventurers have written books about rowing the Atlantic Ocean, but I've never been interested in doing so. My short walks in India and Spain were no great feat, but something about them intrigued me enough to tell the stories in books. My ego didn't play a part in either of those decisions.

Almost for as long as I have been a Working Adventurer, I have been conscious not to believe my own hype that I am amazing and that adventure is the be-all and end-all of life. I am aware that over time the tales I tell are often polished (for simplicity or effect) to within an inch of the truth. So I try to imagine that a peer who I respect is sitting at the back of the room with his Bullshit-ometer held high to cool my bluster and temper the temptation to exaggerate.

There are billions of people on earth whose days are challenging enough without adding the artifice of adventure, and whose lives are not so plump with luxury that they feel a yearning for simplicity and fresh air. And every day, I pass men and women in the street who fare better than me with the ongoing trials and tribulations of real life. I really do not have to try to keep my ego in check at all.

WHAT ADVENTURE WOULD YOU LOVE TO DO, BUT HAVEN'T GOT THE BOTTLE, SKILL SET OR FUNDS TO DO?

- A first ascent of a massive mountain.
- A solo sailing circumnavigation of the world.
- Walking through the Darien Gap and across the Bering Strait to join up the gaps in my round the world bike ride.
- A flight to the moon.
- A return journey to the South Pole, unsupported, from Scott's hut on the coast.

What would you do if it wasn't made public?

If nobody knew what I was up to, I would still have done almost everything I have done in my life, in almost exactly the same style. Indeed, this exact question is one that I often ask myself as a way to check my motivations and help me do the right thing.

When I begin planning a new trip, I filter my ideas to eliminate the madcap and the excessively narcissistic. It is important to clarify my motivations for doing an adventure. It should be fun, or at least fun in hindsight. It has to be personally worthwhile and fulfilling. I have never been worried about pursuing world firsts. More important for me is to ask whether an idea is fresh, new, challenging and exciting for *me*? And in that vein, I always ask myself if I would still make the trip if nobody else ever knew about it?

I began asking this question after a misadventure in Iceland. I was dithering over whether to packraft down a long stretch of fierce white water in a narrow canyon. I wanted to do it, but I sensed it was far too dangerous for my skill level. But then I thought, 'This will look so cool on YouTube', and therefore decided to go for it. I paddled into the rapid, terror mounting. As soon as I hit the white water, I knew that I had miscalculated and made a terrible decision. The raft flipped within seconds, and the water was strong and grey and fast and cold. I nearly drowned but eventually managed to drag my chastened, bedraggled little ass to the riverbank. At which point I noticed that I had forgotten to press 'record' on the GoPro camera!

Would I have taken such a reckless risk in a remote wilderness had I known that nobody would ever watch the footage and applaud me? Absolutely not. It was an important lesson learned.

Some years ago, I was invited to take part in a ridiculously crazy, hardcore expedition. The guy who asked me was someone I admired. I was flattered. I was excited. If we pulled this project off, it would make a brilliant story. I was also scared. It was an extremely dangerous plan. Misery and suffering were guaranteed, though that was part of the appeal. In those days, I rated my ability to suffer and saw it as a point of differentiation and a badge of honour.

Yet, something stopped me from agreeing to the plan. The more

I thought about it, the more I realised that my excitement came almost entirely from how much I would enjoy showing off about the achievement afterwards.

'Would I do this if nobody ever found out?' I asked.

The answer was, 'No.'

I turned down the invitation.

Asking 'would I do this is if it wasn't made public?' is a good question for me to ask myself. I want my journeys and creative projects to be something that I enjoy and care about regardless of whether they have an audience or not. The process itself ought to be reward enough. If I write for an audience's applause, I will only be disappointed when not everyone loves it. If I write in search of adulation (through sales, comments or likes), I will be left craving a little bit more next time.

Writing a book takes so long, earns so little (per hour of work) and is such a flipping painful experience that, first and foremost, I have to write it for myself as a way to digest all the thoughts in my head and feel satisfaction at finally typing 'The End'.

WHY DO YOU ALWAYS GO ON ABOUT HOW YOU WOULD MAKE MORE MONEY AND BE MORE SUCCESSFUL IF YOU DID MORE BIG EXPEDITIONS?

I didn't realise that I do this, but I think it comes down to insecurity. Even when microadventures started to become popular, I always wanted to be regarded as a 'proper' adventurer. People were buying bivvy bags and heading out on microadventures of their own. My income and audience were increasing. But I still wanted to do something epic again to impress other people (and myself).

It took me years to realise that the impact of microadventures was more significant than anything I could manage by striving to be the latest rugged explorer going on big expeditions.

So I apologise if I bang on about my previous big adventures too often. Go sleep on a hill, folks.

What do you miss when you look at your peers who took a more 'normal' route in life?

The aspect of being a Working Adventurer that I could really live without is the constant pressure, both real and self-inflicted, to be continually interesting, original, relevant and enviable (if only online). I hate that a large chunk of my identity and how I feel about myself is linked to online approval. I don't like that my income is hitched to those approval levels. I'm not a President angling for re-election; I am a free spirit who wants to cycle to a café and have enough money in my pocket to treat my friend to breakfast. I would like my working life not to have to depend upon public approval and an endless string of attractive plans. This is a major driver in my increased focus on quietly writing books.

What else do I miss when I look at friends with more normal careers?

- Pensions and sick pay.
- The tacit acknowledgement that someone has a 'proper job' which doesn't need justifying.
- A clear structure of promotion and progression.
- An obvious boundary between 'work time' and 'not work time' so that I could fully appreciate my free time rather than fretting that I should somehow be using it to do something related to my work.
- The camaraderie of working with bright, inspiring colleagues.
- Being able to go on a bike ride without feeling compelled to turn the experience into a pithy blog post about the meaning of life.
- Mentoring and professional feedback.
- Expense account credit cards and the excuse to meet friends after work for a quick drink now and again.

HOW DO YOU KEEP A HEALTHY MINDSET AND REMAIN PRODUCTIVE?

I don't always manage to keep upbeat in my working life. But I know what triggers me to slump, and I know what works to pick myself up again: exercise lots, get into nature and tackle projects that excite me with a clear timetable and a tight-ish deadline.

Do you struggle with feeling isolated or like you're not living your days to the fullest when you are doing the behind the scenes work?

How you would feel about spending most of your working hours alone and left to your own devices will help determine whether the life of a Working Adventurer is for you or not. Some would find it boring and lonely. Others would be totally unproductive; it is no place for slackers. There is no camaraderie, no sounding board to help you unpick professional puzzles, nobody holding you to account. Perhaps spending so much time travelling alone has inured me to all this, for I have never struggled with any of it. I often go for weeks at a time without having a single meaningful conversation about my work. I am often lonely, but never during work hours. I'm too busy and immersed in exciting projects.

I am happy with my own company in my shed and don't feel isolated there. I talk out loud to myself. I choose the music, and I sing and dance. I pace around the shed while I think (a bonus of using a standing desk). I feel a boyish pride in my flatulence rather than shame. But I also love the times when I collaborate with bright people who challenge me and make me think differently. I want to find more opportunities to work with others.

I relish the times when my work overlaps with hanging out with interesting people. This can range from spending a couple of months in extremely close quarters on an expedition, charging around like a lunatic for a few days with a film crew, (high on caffeine, ideas and a ridiculously tight schedule), to simply chatting with thoughtful characters for my podcast.

I struggle with doing work that does not feel worthwhile, when the drag of ennui wrestles the lure of the paycheque. I would find it impossible to work for a company unless I was passionate about its mission. Millions of pounds would not tie me to a tedious job for very long. I don't enjoy the days when I am only doing something for the money, merely trading some hours of my life for some cash.

As well as the usual 'To Do' lists, I have also benefited from having a 'Not To Do' list. It makes me aware of all the things I hate doing and which suck the joy from my shed.

The days when I feel I am living life to the fullest never involve answering emails. They are inevitably those when I am outside in beautiful wild landscapes. There are also days alone in my shed that can compete with that feeling. These are the times when I am producing something good that I know will last for a long time. That knowledge stretches the satisfaction of one day's effort out into many days to come.

Over time, I have manoeuvred into a fortunate position where I can be more selective about the work I take on. Whenever possible, I try to prioritise projects that feel fulfilling, have longevity, and that I enjoy.

ARE YOU HAPPY?

63% of adults are happy, apparently, so statistically I'm likely to be content. The trouble for ambitious folk with eternal *wanderlust* and *fernweh*, is that we always reckon we can find something better over the next horizon and should strive for more out of life than that satisfied 63%...

Did you have to shut down one identity in order to step into this one fully?

Like every career (and life), things work much better when you don't have to pretend to be something you are not. There is a temptation to imagine what an adventurer *should* be like and strive for that image, imitating those I consider successful.

But funnily enough, I ditched that notion on my very first morning of cycling round the world. Feeling overwhelmed by the stupidity of what I had got myself into and crying as I pedalled, I decided that I wasn't going to hide this aspect of the experience. If readers were disappointed by my lack of an explorer's stiff upper lip, then too bad.

Reflecting back, I am interested that I was so matter of fact about this, given that for my entire life I had always been so desperate to fit in, to belong and not to stand out. I don't know why I was suddenly willing to be open and vulnerable with those feelings, but I am glad that I did.

Becoming a Working Adventurer has been, at times, like becoming a teenager all over again. There was a lot to figure out and plenty of awkwardness, missteps and ill-advised hairstyles. I felt embarrassed by the notion of self-promotion. Without it, however, you can't be a Working Adventurer, so you have to either suck it up and get on with it, or go and find a proper job. Occasionally, whilst finding my feet, I became too thrusting, earning a well-deserved smackdown from one gnarled old climber:

> 'A lot of folk find this type of self promotion over the top. Might sit alright with folk who don't know much but there are thousands of folk doing real adventures and just getting on with it. You are obviously highly motivated and talented to your causes but take a tip from me: such statements only throw egg on your face. Sorry to be brutally honest but better you get feedback than think such things are cool. You don't need to do this; you have an impressive CV. Just enjoy it for yourself.'

Through trial and error, I got to a position where I think the tone of my output reached an acceptable balance between being authentic and being loud enough to be noticed. (Correct me if I'm wrong!)

Whilst I would not go so far as to say that I shut down parts of my identity, I do very much separate the strands of my life. As long ago as 2009, I began only posting adventure-related material on my blog rather than any old tidbits that interested me or anecdotes about what I was up to. I only tell the world about certain aspects of my life, not what I had for lunch (re-heated mushroom risotto, since you ask), what I'm wearing (jeans and novelty Christmas elf slippers), who I vote for (Green), my house, my family or anything else that is not relevant to the Working Adventurer side of my life. I don't have any personal social media accounts, not even ones restricted to my real-world friends and family. I have tried to be frank in this book, but I have also been careful to limit that openness only to my work and adventures.

From about the age of 30, I settled upon an identity that was successful in my speaking work and online content. It was a combination of adventure styles, ethos and output that worked well. But I made the mistake of not allowing that identity to evolve as I changed. By the time I hit 40, the disconnect was jarring. I still considered 'success' as an adventurer to revolve around pushing yourself to the limits on major expeditions. Yet not only was I unable to find the time to do those anymore, I realised that they did not excite me as much as they used to either.

Belatedly, I began thinking carefully about what living adventurously meant to me now, settling upon an updated definition that worked better for my current life (and ended up going busking, to my great surprise.)

The growing-up metaphor works well here because, in my work as in my personal life, I eventually grew into accepting who I was and who I was not, what I was good at and what was best left alone. I have slowly grown into the identity of accepting being myself: both in my Working Adventurer life and in the strands of my life that are not played out on the internet.

It has been a relief to no longer feel that I had to play a scripted reality-show version of myself. I had never given much thought to the truism advice of 'be yourself', but it is actually powerful and liberating; not only to *be* yourself but also to be content with what that is.

Aside from the sheer madness of feeling that you somehow should fake an adventurous identity, there is the win-win bonus that you will be more successful if you are authentic and honest as you tell compelling stories and build a viable audience. There is no need, thankfully, to put on an act to impress people.

WHERE DO YOU FEEL AT HOME?

Anywhere far from home.

How do you deal with post-adventure blues and having to come back to normality?

You know that feeling when you return from a long, muddy run? One of those where you get so lost that it goes on for an hour longer than intended and becomes a bit of an epic? Eventually, you find your way home, get warm again and then fall into the soft, welcoming embrace of your sofa with a bucket of tea, a loaf of toast and Test Match Special on the radio.

You have earned the right to lie on your sofa. You replay the satisfying memories from the run. You're proud of yourself, but you feel absolutely no compulsion to get up and run any further. That is what coming home from an adventure feels like. It is delicious. The long-dreamed-of holy trinity of hot shower, cold beer and soft bed never ceases to feel absurdly wonderful.

The trouble is that the gloss soon fades.

For many years, I held onto the false hope that just one more adventure, a really big one, was all I needed to at last heave Excalibur from the stone, scratch the itch, feel content forever and never need to go away again...

Alas, not yet. And, I suspect, not ever.

Embarking on an adventure is like opening Pandora's Box. A new world of possibilities bursts forth. For the rest of your life, you'll have new benchmarks for words like 'excitement', 'endeavour', 'simplicity' and 'purpose'. Ordinary life afterwards can be stifling and frustrating by comparison. Nobody knows the distant places you have returned from. Nobody understands. Nobody can empathise. Nobody cares (which I understand: 'Hang on, you're moaning because you've just been away in paradise having a lovely time?'). This sometimes leaves you a step removed from the people in your life, out of sync, and distant.

Too often, I compare my average days to the salad days of my big adventures. I sometimes find parts of normal life almost too boring, too banal to bear after tasting the freedom of solitude, the intensity of trust and companionship, the beauty and self-examination of wild landscapes, the abundance of time and space, the focused purpose of striving for a goal, the intense appreciation of luxury that is a warm sleeping bag in a frozen tent or a cold mountain stream on a hot day, the moments of living on my wits, the adrenaline and terror of sinew-straining effort, and the spoon-licking frugality of expedition rations or the heady abundance of camping beneath a laden wild avocado tree.

Seen through adventure's dazzling prism, my everyday highs, fitness, prospects, freedom, and independence, my daily levels of contentment and satisfaction all struggle to live up to those highwater marks. The problem is exacerbated by the phenomenon of the focusing illusion, which tends to forget all the boring, horrible parts of expeditions and remember only the high points.

Rolf Dobelli writes in *The Art of The Good Life* about 'the trap of the remembering self. Running barefoot across the USA or conquering Everest in record time can only be considered wonderful experiences in retrospect. At the time, they're torture. Extreme sports feed memory at the cost of moment-by-moment happiness.'

Having worked so hard during the adventure and devoted such energy towards one simple (but not easy) goal, it can feel disjointed to cross a finish line, stop abruptly, have a cup of tea and then think, 'Now what?'

The lack of direction can lead to a feeling of aimless drift. The tangled web of complicated commitments and tasks that make up real life may feel more difficult and less self-gratifying than the one mad mission you had been focused on.

Fulfilling an ambition and achieving something that feels personally meaningful does not necessarily guarantee lifelong contentment. The crux of the issue is often that, 'no matter where you go, there you are'. Running (or cycling) away is not going to resolve that. Any problems you run away from are still here, waiting for you, and all the more vexing for remaining unsolved. Going off into the yonder to slay a dragon of an expedition does not mean that anything or anyone is different when you wake up back home in your bed. On Desert Island Discs, cyclist Sir Bradley Wiggins talked about the comedown after winning the Tour de France or Olympic gold. 'I'd achieved this thing… and it was like, "What do I do now?" It doesn't feel how I thought it was going to feel.'

One of the reasons I began travelling the world was because I was disillusioned with life and thought there must be more to it. This restlessness has driven generations of men and women to achieve bold and marvellous deeds. When I am here, I want to be there.

Whilst away on an expedition, I wrote this in my diary. 'I missed many things, even after so long away from home. Family, friends, a girlfriend and familiarity. To know where I would sleep each night. To have food in the fridge, an income, beans on toast. Barefoot breakfasts, Saturday mornings and sport on TV. Cereal, toast, newspapers. Knowing how the remote control works. The postman. Salad. Toast. Coffee. Ice cream. Running through the rain across the moors. Football matches, mud and friendship, and vicarious hopes and fears on the terraces. Cricket, summer evenings and warm walks home from the pub in dark. Text messaging a meeting point, laughing about the night before. I miss all that. But I will miss all this so much more.'

Whilst busking across Spain, I lay down for a siesta one afternoon on a shaded wooden bench in a cobbled plaza, my toes tickled by geraniums in a window box. I looked up at the blue sky and thought to myself, 'This is the happiest I have been in many years.'

The happiness came not simply from being on a cracking adventure. It came from being on a cracking adventure whilst also realising that my life at home was beautiful too. I was, for once, not running, not seeking something better. I was just lying on a bench on a sunny afternoon, and I was happy.

Adventurers. We may look and dress like bums. We do many things that bums do, and we wish that we were bums. But actually, most of us who go off in pursuit of the expedition life are very unlike bums. We are hardworking, driven, ambitious and conscientious, like good civil servants. Yet, we are also restless, impatient and somewhat full of ourselves.

If these are the traits that pushed you out the door in the first place, you're unlikely to fare well if you return from your adventure, pull on a suit and tie and take yourself off to be a civil servant with your fingers crossed that real life's going to work out just fine now.

If you want an interesting life, go on a huge adventure. But I wouldn't necessarily advocate that path if you're looking for peace or to solve the problems in your life. As the old curse cautions, 'May you live in interesting times.'

I know that not every adventurer feels this way, and I admire those who switch successfully between the different compartments of their lives. There are many similar iterations of my experiences though, told online by many other adventurers, including Anna McNuff, Beau Miles, Ben Saunders, Cal Major, Dave Cornthwaite, Emily Chappell, Juliana Buhring, and Sarah Outen. (I have collated their accounts into one blog post: www.AlastairHumphreys.com/dealing-finishing-big-expedition.)

Being a Working Adventurer does not help with the pursuit of peace after adventures. If, for example, I became a farmer, I suspect that the memories of my adventures could rest as happy ornaments on the mantlepiece of my mind whilst I busied myself with the challenges and goals of my new identity. I would not be so bound to who I used to be. But because I tell the same tales time and again to pay the bills, there is no closure to a story, only dilution and simplification. My present and future are constantly held up in comparison to my past.

But if those are the problems I face, what about some solutions to life's problems after adventures? Solutions are more interesting than problems.

More than anything else, microadventures have been the solution to my post-adventure blues. For the adventures themselves and the brief doses of wildness and adventure, certainly, but also for teaching me to choose to see positives and opportunities in every situation and find a dose of adventure wherever I look. If you don't have time to sleep on a hill (in which case, by the way, you need to make time to sleep on *two* hills), then a lunchtime tree climb is a small step in the same direction as crossing a glacier in Iceland. It is still doing something physical, offline and connecting with nature under the wide and wild sky.

The regular, short, local, cheap microadventures I squeeze around the busy rhythm of my ordinary life have often restored my soul over the past decade. They help me temper my expectations for daily life and encourage me to savour where I am right now. My past is nothing but memories and pictures in my mind; my future nothing but hopes and imaginary visions. Right here, right now, is all that I ever genuinely have. I should therefore treasure it.

After jotting down these thoughts on a village bench under a large beech tree somewhere on the outskirts of London, I finished my coffee, put away my notebook and climbed back onto my bike to ride home. I plugged in my earphones and hit 'shuffle'. Music has the surgical knack of slicing through your memories to precise moments in your life.

The first song that came on was 'Weak Become Heroes' by The Streets. Whoosh! I'm suddenly back under a bridge, somewhere in central Japan, sheltering from the rain. I am soaked to the bone, still skinny and weary from a winter in Siberia. Nothing but grey concrete. Pylons. The neon lights of indecipherable Japanese convenience store signs. I sigh, shiver and plug in my earphones. I rarely listened to music back then: I had only a dozen MiniDiscs to choose from, and chances to recharge my batteries were rare. So I only allowed myself the escapist delight of music when I was either really happy or really struggling.

I click in the new MiniDisc I'd been given in Tokyo, press play and begin to ride. As always, my pace picks up with the beat, my weariness forgotten as I spin the pedals automatically. I'm riding a quiet country road through endless rice fields, zipping through puddles under gloomy skies. The story-telling cleverness of *A Grand Don't Come for Free* transfixes me. The drama of Mike and Simone and his missing thousand quid unfolds as I pelt through the rain, grinning and whooping at the sheer bloody wonder of being on the far side of the world and free as a bird. I have no idea where I'll sleep tonight. My tent is still wet from yesterday; I will be damp again tonight. I am sick of instant noodles, and I cannot read a single word of the local language. Yet still, what a magical privilege a long adventure is.

Now, years later, middle-aged and homeward bound on this cold, blue spring day in England, I understand that the joys of my past adventures still smoulder within me. They bring me happiness when memories like this reappear. Music and bikes and the freedom of the open road will always fill my soul with joy, even here, just an hour or two's ride from home and hurrying to get back in time for the school run.

I smile, sing out loud and hammer homewards, swerving around broken bottles and empty cans with 'Weak Become Heroes' playing in my ears. It is a song recalling the dizzy heights of younger years and the exaggerated polish of your unique and precious memories. For Mike Skinner of The Streets, that meant everyday antics and mid-90s rave culture; for me, it's instant noodles in damp tents.

I am living the second half of the song these days: years have gone by and we are older, looking back. My life's been up and down since those days but, mirroring the song, I have ended feeling that the stars have aligned; we all smile and we all sing.

These can be good times too, even without my big expeditions of old. They are good times made even better by my Pandora's Box stuffed with memories.

HOW ARE YOU?

I'm OK, thank you. I am lean and active, and in good health. I am doing a relatively decent job of accepting what I cannot alter, being grateful for the good things, being brave enough to change what I can and keeping busy with projects that excite me. How are you?

Do you think in the long term or the short term?

In terms of my career, I've always been comfortable knowing that it takes years to grow and establish things. Most of the sales of a book will come in the long tail of years to come, rather than in the breathless, brief spike of launch week.

But in terms of getting on with projects, I take a very short term approach. If I have a good idea, I want to begin it immediately, launch straight in and see how it goes, rather than doing any long-term planning and weighing up the pros and cons.

Perhaps this means that I am impatient but persistent?

I do most of my planning year by year. I tend to pick a project and a book to tackle over the course of a year. In my final week in the shed, I always do an annual review before shutting my laptop for the Christmas holiday. If you search online, you will find templates that guide you through the process of doing an annual review. I first got the idea from Chris Guillebeau's website. I also do what Tim Ferriss calls a Past Year Review to help clarify my thinking.

I blitz my email inbox to empty it, with every message either answered or deleted. I finish all my outstanding tasks then sit down in my shed for two or three days with a notebook, lots of coffee and no internet. I reflect on the year that has passed and make plans for the year to come. I think in terms of categories for my life: Writing, Speaking, Adventures, Fitness, Personal, etc. I brainstorm how each of those categories has gone this year and what I would like to achieve next year.

After pages and pages of scribbling and reflection, I try to condense everything into a concrete, workable plan ready for me to launch into in the new year. I also email all my conclusions to myself using Gmail's Schedule Send function so that they'll pop into my inbox next December when it is interesting to look over them once again and see how I fared. It is a very helpful process.

I suspect that whether this all sounds like long term or short term planning will depend on how you approach your own life.

HAVE YOUR TRIPS MADE YOU MORE BALANCED IN HOW YOU SEE YOURSELF?

Travelling is a brilliant way of teaching you about the world and yourself: your strengths, weaknesses, biases, preconceptions and deeper motives and priorities. I am neither as pathetic nor as tough as I once thought I was. It is a fine education.

Do you ever feel like you must keep adventuring? Do you get tired of it?

It sometimes feels that I am only as good as my answer to the question, 'what's next?' I hate that. I have felt it as a pressure on my life for many years.

I interviewed explorer Ed Stafford about this issue for my book *Grand Adventures* after he walked the length of the Amazon from source to sea. He said:

'I still find it extraordinary that you can do something that no human has ever done before, and people just consume that bit of information and then move on to what you're going to do next. It's like, who said I'm going to do anything next? I might just go home and have a cup of tea. I personally think that, in terms of massive expeditions, if I haven't proved what I wanted to prove to myself by walking two and a half years through the Amazon, then I'm probably going to be forever chasing it if I don't look for a slightly different option. I think to try and do a bigger expedition, then a bigger expedition, and then a more dangerous expedition isn't the way to prove that to yourself. I think everyone needs to not allow chapters of their lives to define them.'

There are certainly times when I would love to end the performing monkey part of being a Working Adventurer. It weighs on me that if I'm to stay 'relevant' and continue earning a living from adventure, I need to keep coming up with clever ideas and shouting about them. If I won the lottery, I would keep going on adventures. I'd keep writing. I'd keep the podcasts. I'd keep doing a few talks, but I would stop the self-promotion and social media.

I am very aware that I am my own golden goose: whilst I keep dancing in the spotlight, everything should be fine. I'll earn enough to keep the wolf from the door. But what happens when the music stops? What happens when my knees are creaky? What happens when I cannot bear to tell the same stories one more time? What will I do next? I don't know yet. Once I stop being interesting, this career is over.

Sometimes I do want to 'go back to normal'. Yet, in this regard, I feel like many a middle-aged person with a mortgage, kids to feed and a fear that changing tack would be folly. I'm sure that I am no longer employable in an office environment. My enthusiasm to work in schools has waned. I don't have many skills beyond the world I work in. If I made a significant change in direction, I would go back to the bottom of the ladder in terms of income, prestige and competence. Of course, if that ladder was a lifestyle that filled me with joy and purpose, it would feel worth doing. However, as I still love my working life, I suspect that I'm destined to be a Working Adventurer forever.

One wearing aspect is telling the same old stories time after time. Some days I have to take a deep breath, strap a smile to my face and remind myself that of course I need to talk about busking or the Empty Quarter. Without such experiences, I am vastly diminished as an adventurer.

I recently had reason to listen to one of my first podcast interviews from way back in 2008. To my horror, I could predict, verbatim, many of my answers a dozen years later because they are still the word-for-word answers I give today! Somebody punch me, please.

I am better at shaking topics up in my talks than many of my adventuring friends who speak on autopilot. Every year I sit down, tear apart the slides that I've used for my presentations and begin again with newer stories and fresh insights. But inevitably, the best stories and the best photos remain. This means that my glory days get reduced to a handful of snaps and regurgitated anecdotes long after the boys of summer have gone.

In contrast, many wonderful experiences get shelved from my repertoire as they don't make for such slick schtick. These then tend to get muscled out of my memory by the noisier soundbites. Either way, I feel that my adventures get diluted either by telling too much or not enough.

Spare a thought then for astronaut Michael Collins who suffered this fate far worse than me after returning from the moon. He thundered:

'If one more fat cigar smoker blows smoke in my face and yells at me, "What was it really like up there?" I think I may bury my fist in his flabby gut; I have *had it* with the same question over and over again.'

Collins worried that he shared with Buzz Aldrin 'a mild melancholy about future possibilities, for it seems to me that the list of exciting things to do here on Earth has diminished greatly in the wake of the lunar landings. I just can't get excited about things the way I could before Apollo 11.' He accepted that there was 'money hanging around, but it is tainted PR money, trading great piles of greenbacks for tiny bits of soul, in an undetermined but unsatisfactory ratio.'

All Collins really wanted to do was 'spend the rest of my days catching fish and raising dogs and children and sitting around on a patio drinking gin and talking to my wife.'

At times I would love to join him.

WHAT ADVENTURE ARE YOU SCARED OF NOT DOING?

So often in life, we worry about the consequences of the things that we do. But only rarely do we fear the consequences of not doing something.

At the moment, I cannot think of an adventure that I am scared of not doing. But the prospect of not living as adventurously as I can scares me. It is one of the biggest drivers in my life. This is connected to the ticking countdown of my life that seems to hang over me more than most people. Right now, this means immersing myself in nature, learning to look, being curious wherever I go, watching the seasons, and living as deeply as I can in my local landscape. These burn stronger in me today than the kind of adventures that lit me up for the past quarter of a century, such as crossing the Sahel, kayaking the Lena or exploring the Chaco wilderness.

How do you stay motivated and focused?

One of the benefits of turning my hobby into my job is that motivation and focus is never an issue. Most of my problems stem from the opposite: I find it hard to step away from my work and concentrate on other things.

I cannot claim that my working days are a whirlwind of laser focus and slick productivity. I'm guilty of wasting time writing amusing Tweets, checking the football results and faffing around online. I fight this by trying to stay offline in the mornings and leaving my phone in the house. I can write well anywhere that does not have the internet or people talking. I am editing these words on a park bench with no power, no watch and no music to distract me.

The website-blocking programme www.Freedom.to (or the Self Control app on Macs) is invaluable for removing the temptation to be distracted. The temptation in itself is a drain on my brain, even when I don't succumb to it. Blocking the internet and keeping my phone in another building is much simpler than wrestling with my willpower.

Rather than fighting negative factors, I work hard to build up positive daily habits. Once something is automated in my head, I don't need to have exhausting mental tussles with myself. I have used a Habit Calendar to help me write regularly, exercise regularly and so on, ticking off each day's accomplishment and building up streaks of successful days. Doing good things every day without thinking about them is much easier than thinking about doing good things every day.

I have never considered this before, but there is a type of pressure when working alone that is probably different from working in a company with many staff. I make decisions on my own that will determine the direction of my work for a year or more at a time. This is a significant percentage of my entire working life, so it important to choose the right projects. Not only must they hold my interest for that long, but they must also result in an output that interests others and earns enough money to be worthwhile. This is what separates a hobby from a job, after all. Should I go on this adventure or that one? Should I write this book or that one? Should I change the focus of my speaking work? Should I record another podcast series even though I don't have a sponsor? It may pay off in future series, but it might just eat up time and money that I should allocate elsewhere.

Once I commit to writing a book, I must then knuckle down to a year of slog whilst also keeping an eye on current cash flow and paperwork. I can imagine that some people would not enjoy this jack-of-all-trades life.

Much of my work is done in six-week sprints between school half terms and holidays. My children are at school for fewer than 200 days a year (maybe I should have remained as a teacher after all?!) which severely limits my writing time. Chuck in weekends, and I simply don't have enough time to indulge in anything less than full-speed ahead work.

I set myself false deadlines to get projects completed. With rare exceptions, I never allow a film edit to drift beyond Friday into next week. When I'm publishing a book, I impose strict deadlines to get the project finished. Almost invariably, this involves at least one night when I do not sleep at all. Foolhardy, perhaps, when I could just do it later at my leisure, but I respond well to pressure (even fake pressure). Pressure helps me get a lot of good work done, quickly. I also use deadlines like Christmas or 'the end of the summer term' as an incentive to get a book finished and available for sale.

I do a lot of my work in batches, particularly repetitive tasks. For example, I did all the grunt work of uploading my podcast episodes over a few days. I could then forget about it all, despite a new episode coming out every week for a year, complete with scheduled blogs and social media posts. Doing it bit by bit over a whole year would have taken much longer overall and distracted my brain regularly.

All of these require a bit of discipline and the establishment of efficient practices and habits. But in the end, the main reason that I keep at it, day after day, alone in my shed, is because I relish the work.

DO YOU HAVE TO KEEP DOING BIG TRIPS TO BE AN ADVENTURER, OR IS IT OK TO LIVE OFF THE LEGACY?

This is one of the conundrums of my life. I feel personal and professional pressure to keep doing new and interesting things. But I'm also aware that whatever I do, people only ever ask me about microadventures or cycling around the world.

What is your backup plan or alternative career path if adventuring doesn't work out or your circumstances change?

It is crucial for anyone wanting to be a Working Adventurer to consider their backup plan. I know that I often toss around gung-ho phrases like 'just do it', 'take risks' and 'be bold', but in the beginning I did all those things with the helpful fallback of being a trained teacher. I knew I could get a job if the adventuring didn't work out.

So be bold, yes, but be pragmatic too. I used to describe my decision to cycle through Colombia at a period of high military volatility as being based on 'pragmatic recklessness'. Minimise and mitigate the risks, absolutely, but at some point you also have to roll the dice. If you are going to take the bold leap to become self-employed and never need to shower again, have you thought through the sensible, practical considerations too?

In terms of what my backup plan is now: I honestly don't know. I no longer want to be a teacher. I don't want to be a pensioner still going around giving talks about my youth. Yet, I have not come up with any realistic alternatives. I want to get into a position where I can write books full time, and writing is more compatible with getting old or ill than adventuring. I have also been daydreaming for many years about becoming a postman on the Shetland Islands...

WHAT'S THE CLOSEST YOU'VE COME TO THROWING IN THE TOWEL?

I have toyed twice with the idea of stopping the work I do and becoming a magazine editor. In the end, I decided against the switch because it felt too narrow for me. Usually, when I get fed up with my work, I just change direction and focus rather than thinking of quitting it all. This probably happens every three years or so. After a lot of time in my shed, working alone, I feel very cut off from the real working world, and I don't really know what other job I might enjoy. Whenever I try to imagine something different, I feel immediate resistance at the thought of being told what to do or even being the boss and having the responsibilities that come with that. I think I am destined to remain in my shed forever, evolving in isolation like Darwin's Galapagos finches until I'm extremely well-adapted for this specific environment, but no other.

Will you keep doing what you're doing?

I sometimes think I've been doing the same thing since I began blogging and adventuring back in 2001. Thankfully, my work has evolved in the past 20 years, though the changes are so gradual I often don't notice the shifting baseline.

As an example of this flux, the adventures I aspired to have arced through gigantic bike rides to elite polar expeditions to sleeping on suburban hills to redefining adventure as playing the violin in public, to spending a year exploring the single small map I live on.

My story-telling has moved from emailing a kind volunteer who manually updated my blog a few times a year (a big FTP palaver) to my first Tweet (March 2008: 'Getting ready for the 120-mile Devizes-Westminster canoe marathon...'), my first YouTube video and recording my first audiobook.

My income has morphed from speaking at primary schools to corporate talks, from self-published books and mappazines to a traditional big publisher and now back to an emphasis on self-publishing. From whooping at receiving free gear as sponsorship to becoming an ambassador for outdoor companies and being paid to wear their clothes.

Writing these paragraphs has cheered me up enormously. It shows me that I haven't just been doing the same thing for 20 years, and therefore there is no reason for the next 20 years to remain the same. Freedom and flexibility are amongst the highlights of being a Working Adventurer.

The times they are always a-changing. My priorities have changed. I feel less ambitious these days and more inclined to ride my bike. Less competitive, more collaborative. Less envious of continent-hopping Instagram travellers, more dreaming of a tight-knit community of friends in the hills or by the ocean. I'm reading more Marcus Aurelius and fewer *How To Market Your Blog* books.

My world is slower and more restricted than it used to be, and I no longer seem to have any answers, only a carousel of questions. During the ghastly year of lockdown, I began going on aimless photography walks. I hoped that meandering might make it easier to pose open questions than my usual manic runs and challenges and missions that all demand solutions. It was an opportunity to examine my working life and untangle myself from the habit or duty of doing things the way I've always done them. To ponder why and how I work and live. To ask whether the things I enjoyed doing in the past are the same as what I want to do in the future. What do I want to spend the rest of my life doing? What do I not want to spend the rest of my life doing? These are not questions to rush.

Asking yourself difficult questions is a good exercise in noticing, slowing down, evolving and adapting to your limitations and constraints – perhaps even turning them into positive virtues. It is an opportunity to reset priorities and simplify needs.

I began by challenging all the assumptions that I have held for a long time about being a Working Adventurer. I consciously considered whether I wanted to hold on to each of them or let them go. I find it harder to let go of expired ways of doing things than to embrace new methods and ideas. Loss aversion theory shows that we all generally prefer to avoid losing something more than we like acquiring equivalent gains. This results in me staggering around with vast armfuls of hoarded ideas and expectations. Shedding some of this load has been extremely helpful.

One evening I opened a double spread of my notebook and titled the left-hand page, 'What annoys me?' and the right-hand page, 'Solutions'. There is no point in being irritated by something if I can find a way to fix it instead.

I also went through every aspect of my life as a Working Adventurer – 'Speaking events', 'My working week', 'Adventures', 'Writing' etc. For each one I allocated various options such as 'Accept it', 'Find alternatives', 'Eliminate', and 'Do more of it'.

This process felt cathartic, like slashing away years of brambles and tangled undergrowth. Wiping everything away and then thoughtfully selecting the few items that fit best with my life right now. This was more clear-cut and satisfying than grabbing an armful of items from a ridiculously over-cluttered attic.

My conclusion from this period of reflection was that I do not intend to keep being a Working Adventurer in the way I've interpreted that model for so long. I am less interested in the thrill of adventure than I used to be, less drawn to tales of endurance or derring-do. I am more interested in the natural world, nature, creativity and encouraging positive change through living adventurously every day. I'm not saying that any of these aspects are better or worse, only that I have changed. Whatever direction a regular reassessment of the way I work leads me in the years to come, I certainly hope that I will keep pursuing paths that are both thought-provoking and interesting.

DO YOU GET BORED SOMETIMES?

I assume the question is about my working life, but you might be surprised how frequently I feel bored when I'm on a big adventure. Plodding down a road all day or hauling on the oars in the middle of a blank ocean is often dull.

By contrast, I don't often feel bored in my daily working life. I could certainly live without those Zoom calls where someone decides to read out their entire PowerPoint presentation. Anything involving the word 'tax' is taxing. I sometimes find writing articles boring, particularly if they are the sort of thing I've churned out many times before. But these thankfully make up a very small portion of my working life.

My Assumptions

I spent some time scribbling long lists about all the assumptions I hold about life as a Working Adventurer. I looked at all the ways I earn money and all the activities I do. I thought about my impressions of an adventurer, and questioned what a Working Adventurer is 'supposed' to do.

Then I sorted these into lists of things that were still relevant and helpful and those which were obsolete, unhelpful or hindering. It was revealing to see all the items I still considered personally important and uplifting listed alongside all the deadwood I have been hauling around with me. I eventually narrowed all my lists down into a few bullet points, which I could pin above my desk to refer to whenever I need to decide the direction I want to go with my work.

It is important to point out that these lists are not right or wrong. They are not the way anyone else should think or act. They were not the way I worked for many years. I am sure that the lists will look different again when I revisit them in a year. The wheel keeps turning.

Assumptions to Abandon

✕ I am an adventurer, first and foremost.
✕ My adventures must define my work.
✕ All the work I do has to have an adventure/outdoor element to it.
✕ Regular social media presence is critical.
✕ Interviews and publicity are vital.
✕ Make the most of my maximum possible hours of work: 9-to-3, five days a week.
✕ I ought to have an element of education in my career.
✕ I need brand partnership roles.
✕ I need regular speaking work.

Assumptions to Keep and Nurture

✓ Spending as much time as possible being active in the outdoors is important.
✓ Living adventurously is my core principle when deciding what to do.
✓ Regular quality online content is important to maintain and grow my engaged audience.
✓ All content should be able to scale up into something that can become passive income, such as podcasts or books.
✓ I need a good answer to 'What's next?' *[I'm surprised this made it into this column, given my dislike of the question.]*
✓ If in doubt, writing books is the most worthwhile use of my working time.

HOW DO YOU DEFINE TRUE ADVENTURE?
Something that you find difficult, daunting, thrilling and new, with a significant risk of failure and a reward that feels worth all the struggle.

What is the biggest professional risk you've taken, and how old were you?

I like this question's specificity. Tim Ferriss wrote that 'life punishes the vague wish and rewards the specific ask.' I was 33 years old when I veered away from my mission to do one big adventure each year. Until then, my hunch had been that I needed at least one new story to write and speak about every year. Other adventurers had demonstrated that this accumulation and progression was a proven career path to tread. So far, I had cycled around the world, run 'the toughest foot race on Earth', walked across southern India and was training for an expedition to the South Pole. Things were heading in the right direction, and I was enjoying it all and benefiting from the self-confidence I was building.

But then I decided to change tack and spend a year doing little trips that I called 'microadventures'. To walk a lap of the M25, go mountain biking with my friends and sleep on many suburban hills. I had an inkling that all the people who enjoyed vicarious tales of big adventure would also love to have more adventures of their own.

But I also worried that some would say, 'Nah, mate. That's not an adventure. That's just camping.' I feared a loss of credibility, something far more terrifying for me than a loss of income. I was concerned that audiences at my talks would not be interested in these little trips. I dreaded that I was slamming the brakes on my adventuring career just as it gained some traction.

The result of all this anxiety and second-guessing? I was named one of National Geographic's Adventurers of the Year (one of the best and most surprising things that has ever happened to me). I signed my first ever book deal with a major publisher, and my career accelerated.

What does this mean? Trust your gut, I guess. Lead don't follow. Don't be afraid to walk your own path.

HOW DID YOU OVERCOME THE FEAR OF ICY COLD AND BAD BACKS SLEEPING IN FIELDS AND FORESTS?

I overcome most of my fears just by having a go. By and large, present fears are less than horrible imaginings. Get a blank piece of paper and start writing. Pick up the phone and say hello. Pack a rucksack ridiculously full with warm clothes and camping mattresses and give it a try.

Do you feel guilty that adventure is an entirely pointless and self-indulgent pursuit with no value to society?

I never felt guilty about adventure when I was young and free, but fatherhood changed my attitude to risk. After becoming a dad, I still craved difficulty, but now I abhorred danger. My interest in extreme expeditions waned. Dying on an adventure would feel inexcusably selfish now. (This selfish side of adventure is explored in *Where the Mountain Casts its Shadow*, a book I found somewhat uncomfortable to read.) Along with the joy and excitement adventure brings, I also feel a stab of guilt about the time I spend away from home, and environmental accountability, which I address in a later chapter.

As a teenager, adventure was thrilling and character building. It got me out of the house and into nature with my friends. In my twenties, adventure became a mission to prove myself to the world and to myself [see: *Moods of Future Joys*]. Adventure was core to my search for a challenging, educated, vibrant life [see: *There Are Other Rivers*. I reckon I can plug most of my books before the end of this chapter!]

The experience of exploring the world led to me wanting to share those lessons with children, so adventure and travel became a vehicle for education [see: *The Boy Who Biked The World*].

Because adventure had such an impact on my own horizons, health and awareness of my potential, I wanted to evangelise about all this good stuff and encourage others to have a go. This was adventure as a transformational experience [see: *Microadventures* or *Grand Adventures*].

With time, my perspective on adventure began switching from physical journeys and expeditions to the creative side of these activities and the critical importance of beginning whatever journey in life you are dreaming of [see: *The Doorstep Mile* or *Ten Lessons from the Road*].

More recently, I have become interested in what the legendary Shane Winser at the Royal Geographical Society has always called 'adventure with purpose'. This means using adventure, travel and expeditions to encourage and showcase positive change in the world [listen: Season 2 of the Living Adventurously podcast].

Far beyond my modest adventures, many expeditions have made a positive contribution to society. Take Jeanne Baret or the Apollo missions as fine examples. Businesses today still learn from Ernest Shackleton when improving their leadership structures. Terry Fox inspired millions of Canadians to get physically active and raise money for charity. Lewis Pugh is both an endurance swimmer and a UN Patron of the Oceans.

Adventure has positive benefits in many areas. There are obvious physical advantages from adventure, whether you are training for an expedition, walking across a country or simply exercising outdoors. Part of successful ageing includes staying active, and hiking, biking, or wild swimming remain appealing even for those who perhaps feel 'too old' for the gym.

The Japanese tradition of *shinrin-yoku*, forest bathing, refers to the meditative, reflective, calming experience of walking in the woods. There is a long history of mental health practices benefiting from nature and therapeutic adventure, including work on depression, anxiety, PTSD and counselling.

Children and adults alike benefit from structured residential adventure programmes, experiential learning, or simply doing their daily work outdoors. Journeys can provide a shared experience to help family well-being and bonding. Outward Bound, an outdoor education organisation, encourages adventures involving uncertainty of outcome, high endeavour and shared experience.

More generally, adventures can play a substantial role in a person's self-development, confidence, spirituality and connection with the natural world. Solo expeditions teach appropriate approaches to risk, commitment and hard work, whilst those with teammates rely upon teamwork, social bonding, empathy, communication and creative thinking. Every challenging adventure also dishes up a healthy portion of humility and self-deprecation.

Some jobs have a clear value in society. Nurses, bin men, librarians, gravediggers. Other people go to work each day and get paid to make the world a bit worse. Factory farming, slash and burn forestry, cigarette manufacturing.

Most jobs have a vaguer impact. If most office jobs disappeared, would the world be a better or worse place? I have no idea, but it is telling that I am even uncertain. What about the musicians, artists and athletes who bring us joy and hope and inspiration and escape? An alien looking down might deem their work pointless or frivolous, but I certainly would not.

And now, tiptoeing out onto thin ice, what about adventurers? Are we pointless, or does adventure play a beneficial role in society? I'm not promoting a vacuous, harmful lifestyle. The damaging footprint of my work is small, all things considered, although I need to reduce it to zero at least, negative if possible. I encourage people to invest in experiences. I think that all this goes to justify myself as being 'not that bad'.

But a Working Adventurer can (and should) encourage a greater appreciation of, and therefore caring for, our health and our planet. I want to do better than 'not that bad'. It is vital that all of us, whatever our profession, make an effort to understand how we are damaging the natural world and take steps to reverse that. Perhaps I should have become a zoologist or work in public health to really make a difference. Yet even an adventurer can act as a useful lever for changing perspectives and priorities. This could impact wilderness conservation, rewilding or responsible eco-tourism, for example, or more diverse fields like obesity, depression and delinquency.

Overall, adventure is the best education I have ever had, and the most fun too. That feels reason enough to encourage others to have a go at it themselves and reassurance that adventure is more than a pointless and self-indulgent pursuit.

HOW DO YOU BALANCE FINDING AMAZING UK-BASED ADVENTURES WITHOUT SPOILING HIDDEN SECRETS?

To help avoid spoiling tranquil places I don't geotag my Instagram posts. I don't include maps or route plans in my blogs or books. Partly this is for conservation reasons, but it's also to encourage independence and serendipity in adventure planning. Hatching your own schemes is much better than following prescribed routes and recipes. They are original, satisfying and help you escape the crowds.

How can we make the world of adventure better?

Looking back on 25 years in adventure, both as a lover of it and in terms of my work, certain aspects stand out as being particularly impactful and rewarding. Searching out new experiences and daring myself to be bolder. Doing things differently and being curious about what that might lead to. Learning to be flexible and to roll with situations. Exploring new lands, reading good writing about great journeys and improving my narrative skills. And above all, trying to live as deeply as possible. I have as much enthusiasm for all this as when I first set out. I certainly have not become jaded by adventure. I still have dozens of dreams and ideas. I will be disappointed and surprised if I don't say the same thing in another 25 years.

I imagine that many of these sentiments will be familiar to all of us who enjoy adventure. Being a Working Adventurer has also brought me closer to some of the thornier problems the adventure world faces. The fact that the question of, 'How can we make the world of adventure better?' has even been asked in this book shows how much has changed since I slurped my first lukewarm dehydrated meal in a damp sleeping bag a quarter of a century ago. Back then, adventure was something you did because you enjoyed it, like playing football or going dancing. I certainly had no notion that there might be anything wrong with it or that it needed improvement.

I am grateful that adventure has been one of the core pillars of my life. So I am certainly not concluding that adventure is broken or something to be embarrassed about. Rather, it is in the nature of most of us who love adventure to strive to improve things and to care for our world.

Back in the day, I believed flying around the world as often as possible was cool, and that buying as much shiny gear as I could afford was awesome. Although a love of the natural world drove my travels, I gave little thought to how I might be damaging it, nor that I might have a role to play in persuading others to take care of the planet too.

And whilst I loved talking adventure with anyone interested, I had no awareness that I was privileged to be going on those adventures. I was fortunate to have the means not only to transport myself to wild places, but also to clothe and equip myself for their conditions. I assumed adventure was only a question of enthusiasm and determination. Had I ever thought about the matter (which I didn't), I would have said, 'The outdoors are open and accessible to everyone. It's not complicated. It doesn't have to be expensive. Just do it.' I probably held an attitude of quiet but snobbish elitism about the type of people who were resourceful enough to make their adventurous plans happen and then tough enough to finish the job.

There is now more depth and nuance to what adventure involves. The damage, the lack of inclusion and the consumption gets rolled in with the thrills, the health benefits, the personal development and the love of nature. There are also many issues involved with adventure post-COVID, such as containing the spread of a global virus, a crippled travel industry, wildlife and habitats that rely on tourism to survive, communities that benefit from travel, vaccination passports, and re-opening of countries.

The responsible adventurer (a perfect title for a zeitgeisty Instagram account) is now concerned about increasing participation, diversity, access for children, the elderly and the disabled, improving biodiversity, ethical outdoor brands, over-consumption, flying too much, getting to net-zero negative impact in the adventures we celebrate and bringing nature to cities and city-dwellers. All that is quite a load to lug up a mountain, particularly when you consider that I used to regard adventure as a carefree pastime like playing football.

Kurt Hahn, the founder of Outward Bound, was way ahead of me. Almost a century ago, he saw compassionate adventure as a solution to these six problems:

- The decline of fitness due to modern methods of locomotion.
- The decline of initiative and enterprise due to the widespread disease of 'spectatoritis'.
- The decline of memory and imagination due to the confused restlessness of modern life.
- The decline of skill and care due to the weakened tradition of craftsmanship.
- The decline of self-discipline due to the ever-present availability of stimulants and tranquilisers.

- The decline of compassion due to the unseemly haste with which modern life is conducted.

If we are to leave the adventure world in a better state than we found it, we could do a lot worse than tackling those challenges. (Incidentally, Hahn recommended four 'antidotes': fitness training, expeditions, projects involving craft and manual skills, and helping with a rescue service such as surf lifesaving or first aid.)

I hope that we can expand the scope of 'adventure' to include not only wilderness experiences (with all their learning, leadership and self-development) but also a spirit of exploration in rural or urban landscapes. Prioritising local adventure over list-ticking jet-setting is vital. There are mental and creative elements to adventure as well as the physical challenges.

Challenges are a significant aspect of adventure, certainly. They help us push the limits of our individual potential. This should be done without ego, exclusion, arrogance or undue consumption. We do not 'conquer' mountains or nature: we live with them and learn from them if we are humble enough to do so. Jasmin Paris' epic, yet modest Spine Race victory on the Pennine Way (a 268-mile, non-stop, winter mountain marathon) whilst still breast-feeding is the sort of challenge we should be championing and emulating – in style and ethos if not achievement level.

I would like to see an increase in the number of those who get out and participate in adventures of their own, inspired by stories such as Jasmin's. A more diverse roster of adventurers will appeal to others like themselves: young and old, more women, more diversity and all doing affordable local adventures that enable more of society to join in. There are already more than enough non-disabled, middle-class, white guys like me telling our tall tales.

We need to find ways to make adventure cheaper and simpler. The increase during lockdown of people walking, running, cycling and exploring their local area was heartening. On some of the paths I run, I saw people for the first time in two decades! How can those of us in the outdoor world connect with all these new families wobbling along on ill-fitting old bikes dug out from the depths of garden sheds and with the young couples tip-toeing through nettle patches in flip-flops and headphones?

It confirms what I have known ever since writing *Microadventures* in 2014: my attempts to encourage folk to take on adventures of their own has very much been preaching to the converted. There are swathes of the population who have only just discovered and benefited from their local pockets of wildness. There are countless more who have not done so at all.

Whether we continue to embrace doorstep adventure and find wonder and satisfaction in it will be up to us as individuals. It comes down to a framing of our attitude. Can the purpose of our exploring be achieved locally and sustainably?

For many years, one subject I steered clear of as a Working Adventurer was the turbulent intersection where adventure overlaps with politics and activism. I stayed quiet because I felt that my mission was simply to encourage more people to have more adventures. I did not want to veer onto other topics or cause alienation or distraction. The most effective way to get a message out is to focus tightly and say the same thing, over and over again, year after year.

Yet, I am slowly raising my head above the parapet. Why? Because I am increasingly alarmed about the impact our (my) behaviour is having on the natural world. Every time I flew to America and back to give a talk, an area of Arctic ice the size of my shed melted. By 2050 there will be more plastic than fish in the oceans. A football pitch-sized area of rainforest is felled every six seconds. Half a million of us climb and erode Snowdon every year. Sometimes I want to cry. Sometimes I want to scream. The least I can do is start to shout a little bit.

All of us who love adventure and nature have to help replenish and improve the natural world whilst also being vocal about its urgency and importance. I hate the word 'influencer', but it is actually spot on. Those of us who become Working Adventurers through growing an audience have a responsibility to show leadership if we are to leave the world of adventure in a better condition than we found it. This includes considering where and how we explore. What is the purpose of our adventures? What will our actions encourage others to emulate?

IF YOU COULD CHANGE ONE THING IN THE WORLD, WHAT WOULD IT BE?

I would get every world leader, business person, and billionaire to spend six months cycling through distant lands. This might make us all less suspicious of 'others' and motivated to work together to tackle climate change and inequality.

How do you think your adventures and your approach to adventure would have been different if you were a woman?

A confession: I put off tackling this question for a long time. It is impossible to answer 'correctly', and whatever I write will be skewed by my own life experience. My answer is sure to generate howls of exasperation from people of all genders who disagree with me. Anyway, enough of the disclaimers. Here is my opinion.

I often get asked about adventuring as a woman. It's not really my speciality, so I always urge the questioner to seek out female adventurers and find out about their personal experiences. There are more and more mad, marvellous women cycling continents, rowing oceans and running over mountains these days, which is brilliant to see. You might begin by reading two anthologies of women adventurers, *Tough Women* and *Waymaking*, or browsing the online Intrepid and Adventure She magazines. Every year I am pleased to see an increase in the number of women involved in adventure. More role models will mean more girls want to try adventures of their own.

If you set aside the hurdles of life involved with getting out onto expeditions, I don't think my wilderness experiences themselves would have been much different as a woman. Men and women alike love wild places, operate competently in them and have magnificent adventures either solo or in teams.

But my adventures in places that involved interacting with other people would certainly have been different as a woman. Sadly, women are much more at risk of assault and unwanted advances than men are. I am sure having that thought in the back of my mind every time I walked home after dark for my entire life would have impacted how bold and trusting I might be on my journeys, and perhaps impacted whether I even wanted to travel at all. It would also have altered my considerations about whether to travel solo or not. I would probably have needed more money for my trips so that I could spend nights in hotels rather than some of the fairly nuts places I have dossed down in, such as a platform on Karachi railway station, an abandoned tower block in Istanbul or a graveyard on the outskirts of Mexico City.

After talking to many women who have travelled widely, I also understand that women do have some advantages on the road. People they meet are generally more kind, inquisitive and welcoming. And women get access to some fabulous people and situations that I will never encounter, particularly in regions such as the Middle East.

It is easier for men to get to the start line of their big adventures. When I first raised the idea of going on adventures, friends worried about my safety, sanity, and sanitation. Some doubtless saw me as eccentric. I am sure that the worries and preconceptions foisted upon an adventurous woman would be far greater. I imagine my family might have been more reluctant for me to leave if I had been a young woman planning to travel solo, wild camp, knock on strangers' doors and not wash for weeks on end.

Anyone who has sat in a meeting with a few men and a few women will know that men are more likely to push themselves (ourselves) forward, to talk loudly and be confident in their all-round awesomeness. This is tedious in meetings but probably helped me have the chutzpah to think, 'I could be an adventurer. I'm going to try something huge and stupid that I am in no way prepared for.' My confidence went even further than that: 'I'm going to contact everyone and tell them what an amazing speaker and writer I'll probably be. They should definitely pay me.'

There is a different weight placed on your image for male or female Working Adventurers, which is not good. If you're a smouldering, rugged hunk of a man, then you're going to get paid more, and more often, than some scrawny ginger guy. But (fortunately for me) it doesn't matter too much if you're no oil painting as a bloke, so long as you're tough or funny or eloquent. The skew is far more significant for women. Their looks and image are scrutinised and commented on much more than mine ever are.

Despite all these barriers, there has never been a better time to be a female Working Adventurer. In terms of working with brands or marketing campaigns, speaking events or TV bookings, if you take a man and a woman who've both done great trips and can tell their story equally well, the woman will be a better commercial pick.

To conclude, and no doubt to the irritation of some readers, I'll say that the world of adventure feels more balanced and equal than many other spheres of life, albeit definitely not perfect. It is a brilliant time to be an adventurous woman, whether you are looking for role models, planning an expedition or becoming a Working Adventurer. Search online for the Adventure Queens, Love Her Wild or the Adventure Syndicate to help you get involved, or seek inspiration from the impressive Tough Girl podcast which has interviewed more than 400 female adventurers.

DO YOU HAVE ANY ADVICE FOR DESIGNING ADVENTURE-RELATED EQUIPMENT?

Ask specific questions to the specific audience you are designing for. It seems clear to me that outdoor designers rarely ask women, for example, what they actually want their gear to look and perform like. I'm pretty sure not many would answer, 'we need our stuff to be exactly like the men's. Just pink it and shrink it, please.'

How do you deal with the dilemma of flying and adventure?

When I reflect on the state of the planet, I feel a mixture of sadness and anger, plus a sense of how tiny and ineffective I am to do anything about it. We have wrecked our home! But there is now an increasing demand for change and the beginnings of individual and collective action. So there is room for hope in my heart as well. Nobody reading this book is unaware that air travel is bad for the environment. Only climate change deniers would argue against a correlation between human behaviour, such as taking flights, and our planet's critical position.

All this was not common knowledge or cause for much mainstream concern until relatively recently. I cannot remember the first time I boarded a plane and thought to myself, 'I'm really excited about visiting this place: it's a shame that my visit is contributing to destroying it.' But it was undoubtedly more recently than I am comfortable with. It is an inconvenient truth that those of us who love exploring wild places are generally in the top swathe of individuals causing the most harm to the world.

I have always loved flying off to new places. I love the departure boards at airports. I love taking off and leaving the drab, familiar world behind. I love looking out of the window for hours at expanses of delicious landscapes or ocean. I love the blast of hot air and new smells when you step out of the plane into a new land. Wanderlust has been a constant throughout my adult life. But the connection between flying and my attitude to climate change has shifted through several stages in recent years.

1. Ignorance. *Flying off to Tamil Nadu marks me out as a curious lover of the world.*
2. Ignoring. *I have learned that flying to New York is harmful. But I have always been desperate to visit and I cannot wait. Oh well. Anyway, adventure is my job. I have to fly. More beer, please.*
3. Guilt. *This is really dumb for me to be flying all the way to Hong Kong in Business Class just to give a talk about the joys of simple*

living and human-powered travel, even though it's exciting, well-paid and good for my ego.

4. Guilt + Offsetting. *I really do want to visit my friend living in a cabin on a Swedish island. So I'll make sure to plant loads of trees to offset my emissions after flying there.* (There are significant problems with offsetting, although it is the least we should do every time we fly.)

5. Action. *I need to decline all invitations for work that require flying unless the circumstances are exceptional. I can take the train to talks in Europe or trips to the Alps. I know that I could do more, such as pledging to go Flight Free entirely. But I can't quite yet make my working self promise that I will never step on a plane again. I will offset my flights, and if I do ever fly beyond Europe for work, I will donate 50% of my fee to environmental organisations. I hope that this results in more good than harm coming from my actions. As the sailor Bernard Moitessier said, 'If you wind up making more than enough for your reasonable needs, you can always spend part of it on things that don't hurt anyone, like planting trees.'*

6. Action + Discussion. *This chapter is a small step towards not only changing my behaviour but also inviting others who love travel to consider their actions and impact.*

I don't know what number you are at on this list, but I'd challenge you to read *The Uninhabitable Earth* and *There is No Planet B*, calculate your personal footprint and not feel moved to step up a number or two.

I have three problems regarding my adventures and flying:

1. I face a moral conflict in that flying harms the natural world I cherish.
2. I face a personal dilemma because I'd love to visit New Zealand and Antarctica, and what difference will it honestly make if little old me doesn't hop on a plane there?
3. I face a professional conundrum because my career would be more successful if I flew to more awesome places.

I think there are three acceptable answers to these problems:

1. If an action causes harm, I should stop doing it.
2. If I'm not part of the solution, then I am part of the problem. The cop-out excuse of being too small to make a difference is perhaps what some random school kid might have chewed over on the day she first decided to skip school in order to protest outside the government buildings in Stockholm. Instead, Greta decided to act.
3. What are my priorities? What is enough? What is success?

Just 1% of the world's population is responsible for half of aviation's emissions. Those of us in that group are doing far more than our fair share of damage. Yet, it is also true that flying makes up only 2.5% of the global carbon emissions that need reducing to zero as soon as possible. A mere 100 companies are responsible for 71% of global carbon emissions. They are the gargantuan problem, not you or me taking an important flight. In some ways it is like worrying about drinking from a plastic straw; what journalist George Monbiot calls 'MCBs' (micro-consumerist bollocks): irrelevant distractions that make us feel better, but only distract from the real problems. Slashing the billions of tonnes of carbon emitted each year to zero must be the responsibility of big business, innovation and government action, with us individuals holding them to account through our actions and our voting.

Of course, flying is not the only way that we harm the planet. We do so every day through our diet, lifestyle (the plastic, steel and concrete we use), the stuff we buy and cars we drive, the energy in our homes, having kids and making voting choices. The words I'm typing are stored in a fluffy-sounding cloud that is actually an energy-guzzling warehouse full of whirring hard drives. I'm sipping a coffee whose environmental impact somewhat sours the taste when I think of it, and writing this on a mineral-rich laptop that will end up in landfill one day.

It is certainly easier for me to reconcile not flying when I already have a memory bag stuffed with the sounds of the call to prayer in Jeddah, the humidity of a midnight train in Pakistan, the Arctic swirl of northern lights or the kerosene lamps and star-filled blackness of a night in a mountain village in Bolivia. I have already travelled a lot (and damaged a lot). It is not very fair for me to fill enthusiastic young adventurers with a sense of *flygskam*, or 'flight shame'. To them, I must apologise for my ignorance and then my later indifference. But moving forwards, we need to act together. The future is in all our hands: either with solutions or with big problems.

So I am not writing this to deter anyone who is excited about a rare big adventure or a cherished holiday. Events like this are a red herring distraction from the need for lasting change in humankind's behaviour. Bear in mind the carbon to reward ratio of your flight, by all means. It is better to fly somewhere and then stay for a long time rather than hop on a short-haul flight for a weekend break with a poor carbon to reward ratio. I would like to challenge those of us who claim to be both Working Adventurers and a lover of the landscapes we play in to formulate conscious conclusions between our actions, the signals we send and the impact on the environment.

Adventurers like me often justify the hypocrisy of damaging the wild places we love by resorting to David Attenborough's argument that 'No one will protect what they don't care about, and no one will care about what they have never experienced.'

There is truth to that, certainly. I came to feel guilty about flying once I learned about the fragility of the places I had come to treasure. It is comparable to the overview effect experienced by astronauts looking back at Earth and appreciating its vulnerability and value. Since beginning to explore the single map that I live on, I have already written twice to my MP about local environmental issues that my meanderings have raised concerns about.

I have an audience that reads what I write. I know that the most significant way I can make an impact is by encouraging people to ask themselves questions. And I am trying to make you care, right now. But how can I do this without preaching or being a hypocrite? Positive solutions such as local microadventures are more effective and less annoying than proselytising from a position of imperfection. I prefer to promote all the great adventures you *can* do rather than chuntering about what you shouldn't do.

So how can I make matters better through my writing? Can I do more than just sing the praises of local, low impact adventures?

I'm aware that the online platform I have built has the potential to generate more positive action than the small amount of harm I avert by not stepping onto an aeroplane. Answers on a postcard, please.

I would love to travel more widely, but my frustration at not flying decreases over time as I discover how exciting it feels to travel to the Alps by train, watching out of the window for the first glimpse of mountains and snow. My favourite way of beginning an adventure is sitting with a friend, a map and a beer in the buffet car of the Caledonian Sleeper train as it pulls slowly out of Euston station bound for the Scottish Highlands. Travelling to talks in Paris or Amsterdam by Eurostar is far preferable to the grim experience of airports and not significantly slower than flying, either. (But it is still much more expensive than flying, which is ludicrous and needs to be remedied ASAP, perhaps through carbon taxes, VAT on airline tickets and aviation fuel taxes. Ideally, the environmental cost of the journey ought to be reflected in the price of the ticket.)

Adventure does not have to depend on flying. My favourite Everest story is of Göran Kropp setting off from his home in Sweden to cycle to Everest and then climb the world's highest mountain. The biggest adventure of my life was a magic carpet ride around our planet by bicycles and boats. I visited Ethiopia, Ecuador, Seattle and Samarkand without needing to fly. You need a heck of a lot more time, yes, but you do not necessarily need a plane to get there. A significant transformative experience in my adventuring life was walking a lap of London and learning to look differently at the landscape I lived in. Forcing constraints onto adventures almost always makes them more interesting.

One of my richest travel experiences was the 'world tour' of Yorkshire I took by bicycle. Flying is not only terrible for the environment and our conscience, but it also consumes a significant percentage of your adventure budget and, for short breaks, a painful proportion of your time away. You often end up wasting a whole day of your trip at each end.

So instead, I spent a month exploring the backroads and bridleways of the county I grew up in, chatting to folk along the way about what living adventurously meant to them. It was an experiment to compare the feeling of crossing continents with crossing a county. I knew more about cycling in the Yukon than I did about cycling in Yorkshire. Yet Yorkshire is where I grew up and where I still consider to be 'home'. Could I find adventure close to home? Could I discover anything new and feel like I was actually exploring? Could a small place satisfy my curiosity and wanderlust in the way that far-off lands have always done?

Yes, yes and yes again! It was a fantastic experience. We have so much to gain from adventuring in a sustainable, sensitive way. It certainly need not be a compromise.

When deciding to spend a whole month cycling only in Yorkshire, my biggest concern had been that even God's Own County might not be sufficiently varied to keep me interested for that much time. Yet, if you can persuade yourself to travel slowly and with curiosity, more and more is revealed to you. I found myself wishing that I had far more time to spend on this journey through what I had anticipated would be familiar scenes in one small corner of my small country tucked away in one small corner of a small continent (on a small planet in a small solar system…). The world is like a fractal. You get one impression by looking at the whole. Zoom in though, and you can glean a comparable wisdom. There are similar experiences and lessons wherever you choose to seek them. The closer you peer, the more there is to see.

There are 8000 rivers in the UK. Do I honestly need more than that? Such abundance, such scope for adventure on my doorstep. If I cycled every street in London, it would, in its own way, be as fascinating a journey as cycling an equivalent 10,000 miles from my front door to Asia and back.

There is a short running film on YouTube that encapsulates beautifully the rewards of exploring locally and thoroughly. Of Fells and Hills encapsulates many of my thoughts about life, adventure and the sense of belonging that comes from localness. One line in the film says, 'There's a point where we're trying to see more and more throughout our lives and it just ends up getting diluted.'

I have learned to relish embracing the constraints that not flying imposes on choosing adventures. It has focused my mindset of exploring closer to home. I am very much learning to agree with the closing line of that small film: 'In the end, I think that a single mountain range is exploration enough for an entire lifetime.'

HOW CAN YOU BALANCE ADVENTURE IN YOUR OWN COUNTRY WITH SUSTAINABILITY? THERE IS SUCH POOR TRANSPORT ACCESS TO THE COUNTRYSIDE.

Stay local, don't geotag (or visit) hotspots and lobby the government for improved, affordable rail travel. The bicycle carriages appearing on a few Scottish trains is a good start.

When did you go vegan, why did you do it, and how easy was it to make the change?

I decided to give a short answer about why I eat a vegan diet as nobody likes an evangelical proselytising vegan. Heaven knows there are enough of them (us) around!

WHEN: After a lifetime of knowing that a lot of animal farming is abhorrent but wilfully ignoring it as I loved steak, kebabs, chicken wings and cheese. After many years of accepting vegetarians but believing that vegans were weirdos. After being ignorant for most of my life about the climate implications of industrially farmed animals. After all this, I belatedly but suddenly turned vegan in 2018. I did it entirely for environmental reasons, although once you start learning about industrial farming, you can't help but be repulsed by its callousness and grossness.

Initially, I only intended to become a vegetarian until I learned about the impact of dairy farming on the environment. I also stopped eating seafood when I discovered that 90% of fish populations are either overfished or fished to capacity. Industrial fishing also accidentally kills tens of thousands of albatrosses each year. And Google 'prawn bycatch' if you want to taint your next delicious plate of barbecued prawns. Several platefuls of other species were likely killed and discarded in the process of catching them. This is the problem with reading lots of books: they can put you off your lunch.

WHY: Whilst there *is* an important role for animals in the global food chain (grass-fed, scraps-fed, marginal land, fertilising, regenerative silvopasture, rotational smallholdings, etc.), there is no doubt that our current animal industry is a massive contributor to the climate crisis, barren oceans, deforestation, desertification and loss of biodiversity.

Every year there is a day known as 'Earth Overshoot Day' which marks the date when our use of resources exceeds what Earth can regenerate in that year. Last year Earth Overshoot Day was on August 22nd. If a friend of yours burned through his annual salary by August and then demanded you bankroll his debt for the rest of the year, you would be horrified. It is literally an unsustainable way to treat our planet.

If you look at the big picture, going vegan is not a complicated decision. Humans have turned an area the size of North America, South America, and Australia combined into farmland. 80% of that area is used for beef and dairy production, much of it to grow food for the cattle. Americans each eat over 110 kilograms of meat a year, and Europeans consume nearly 80 kilograms (compared to a handful of kilograms per Indian). The world, quite literally, is not big enough for everyone to behave as we do.

I decided to do my bit to help in the simplest way I could, right now: opting out of that industry and its impact. The planet is screwed, and immediate, massive, universal change is needed. With that backdrop, the least I can do is swap tonight's spag bol for a delicious vegan chilli which even my very suspicious dad ate without grumbling about the lack of meat. (The recipe was Anna Jones' 'Proper Chilli' if you're curious to Google it.) We all say that we would do anything for our children, but we say it whilst cheerfully chomping a cheeseburger.

HOW EASY: Once I committed to it, I found it far easier than I imagined to adapt my diet. Buying a new recipe book was helpful in re-learning how to cook and crucial in continuing to love mealtimes. If a new habit remains a chore, it will sooner or later fail. I have successfully recommended *The Green Roasting Tin* recipe book to carnivores and plant munchers alike.

Meat eaters are often curiously obsessed with how vegans can 'get enough protein', even those who pay scant attention to their own percentage intakes of protein, fat and carbohydrate. I prioritise proteins when planning my meals, but only in the same way that I used to think, 'I'll cook that chicken and find some veg to go with it'. I have noticed no impact in my new diet on my energy levels, double bodyweight deadlifts, or 15-mile runs.

I find that I miss eggs more than meat, and I allow myself to eat them when they come from someone's happy garden chickens fed on kitchen scraps. I have no problem either with someone going fishing or hunting to catch their next meal if done sustainably and compassionately. I also eat meat (or whatever I am served) in other people's homes. Hospitality and generosity eclipse my opinions on the way I choose to eat.

This is, of course, a long, complicated and emotional subject. I have offered a brief, simplified answer from a neophyte. But whether you agree or disagree with me, I'd urge you to read these books and consciously decide whether it is better for the planet for you to eat meat or not:

- *Eating Animals* and *We are the Weather: Saving the Planet Begins at Breakfast* by Jonathan Safran Foer
- *The Uninhabitable Earth* by David Wallace-Wells
- *The Omnivore's Dilemma* by Michael Pollan

HOW CAN I EAT BETTER?

'Eat food, mostly plants, not too much.' – Michael Pollan

WHAT IS THE ONE CEREAL BAR YOU TAKE ON YOUR ADVENTURES?

I don't eat cereal bars. My favourite snack for a microadventure is always a banana, made even better now that I have a plastic yellow banana guard. (You'll find banana armour filed in my life under 'Mocked Before Converted' along with running tights, SatNav, mobile phones, deadlifts and almond butter.)

What are you most excited about this year?

This year I am excited about the approach of summer. With each passing year, I crave more and more the warmth, light, and colour of summertime. If you are reading this in the summer, know then that I am looking forward to the autumn colours. If it's winter, I will be anticipating spring's green shoots. And, at any time of the year, I'm looking forward to snow.

I am excited about time in the hills, sleeping under the stars, swimming in rivers, canoeing with my friends, watching waves and walking in woodland. I am looking forward to reading the next horizon-shifting, world-changing book that crosses my path, cheering live sport and going to the pub to reminisce about adventures or a café to spread out a map and plan new journeys.

In terms of work, I am excited about my continuing experiments with self-publishing books. I would love to record another podcast series. Right now, I am eager to reach the final read-through of this manuscript and launch *Ask An Adventurer* into the world.

As well as being excited about everything I want to do in the next year, I have also enjoyed the process of challenging my assumptions and cutting back on aspects of being a Working Adventurer. So I am eager to appreciate what I will *not* be doing and curious about what I will choose to do in their place. I am making space for other things to happen. But right now, I fancy going to the pub with my friends to throw around bold ideas and new projects. I'll meet you in the garden of the Red Lion tonight. Drinks are on me!

IS IT BETTER TO ADVENTURE WHILE YOU ARE YOUNG, THEN SETTLE DOWN AND HAVE TO REMEMBER ALL THE GREAT THINGS YOU DID, OR IT IS BETTER TO ADVENTURE LATER IN LIFE AND ESCAPE YOUR ESTABLISHED ROUTINE?

I'll avoid the spectre of 'woulda, coulda, shoulda' sadness by saying that I think it is always better to adventure as soon as you get the opportunity in life. You might get more chances later on as well. Delaying adventures hoping that you'll have some fine times later on is not the way I like to live.

Of course, this is all very well if you can do it, but it is not realistic for many people. So my answer is not 'travel while you're young' but 'travel as young as you can', dependent upon your circumstances. Then do your best to savour the memories later on rather than allowing them to taint your later years and make them feel drab by comparison.

What advice would you give yourself if you were starting out today?

- If possible, do not delay your adventure dreams.
- Get strong, run fast, ride far, walk long. Make the most of your youth. (Which, of course, you won't, because nobody does.)
- Push yourself physically hard whilst you are young. Your fondness for suffering will fade before your fitness or stamina does.
- As I wrote in *The Doorstep Mile*, 'When you are young, you're too young. When you're old, you are too old. When you are broke, you can't afford it. When you have a little money, you want a little more. Before you begin, you have no idea what you are doing and need to learn more. Before you begin, you have no momentum. There will always be one more item on the To-Do list before you are ready. Simply put, it is never the perfect time to begin. Instead, we kick the can of our cherished but elusive dreams down the road until 'the time is right' while simultaneously pushing the wasted years out of our mind.'
- You will never have as much spare time as you do now. Use it.
- Always try to keep the viability of your adventure dreams in your own hands.
- Travel cheap, travel far.
- Travel more slowly than you are inclined to do.
- If in doubt, strap a tent to the back of a bicycle, pedal away from your front door and see how far you get.
- Go on journeys of authenticity and substance. Go epic, go original, go thought-provoking.
- Look for ways to use your adventures to educate, inspire or at least entertain.
- Ask yourself what is the purpose of your adventures beyond 'willy-waving'.
- Seek out places and cultures you know little about.
- Travel alone to learn about yourself. Travel with a friend to learn empathy and consideration.
- Pushing yourself to your physical and mental limits occasionally is priceless.
- Don't accept a crap editor. The search for a good editor is as elusive

and rewarding as pursuing a unicorn. When you find a good editor, hang on tight to them.

- Write for yourself. Write something *you* are proud of. If you do that, then you shouldn't worry about sharing it publicly.

- Find a few friends whose opinion you trust. Dare yourself to show them your early work. Ask them for honest feedback.

- Writing a book is ferociously difficult. I only ever manage it by forcing myself to write 1000 words every day.

- Heed Anne Lamott's 'shitty first draft' rule. Of course, your early writing is rubbish. Just keep going.

- What do you know more about than anyone else in the room? What niche are you an authority in? How can you help others in that niche?

- Imagine you are at a large and noisy dinner party. You need to talk occasionally and be interesting or entertaining. But you mostly need to listen to others, answer questions and be helpful. Aim for roughly the same proportions on social media.

- Don't just show off about yourself and your life. (Although, alas, you will have to do some of this. Try to do it with decency at least.)

- Decide which online platforms you want to focus on. Work hard on these, then use automation to duplicate your efforts widely across other platforms. Each social media platform has a different vibe, so duplication is not as good as tailoring your efforts for each one. Then again, spending all day behind a computer is not as good as being out on adventures.

- Remember that today's popular social media platform may be tomorrow's nostalgic laughing stock. Don't put all your efforts into one platform, and always build content on your own website.

- Get efficient so that you can get back outside.

- Produce better content, not more content.

- To make a living from writing books, you need to be either prolific or brilliant.

- Knuckle down to writing. It is hard work. Treat it as such, not as a luxury to dabble with when the muse strikes.

- Be proud, but not too proud of your Amazon 5-star reviews. Laugh at your 1-star reviews. Worry about your 3-star reviews. I'd rather have 51 great reviews and 49 stinkers than 100 readers saying, 'It was OK.'

- Simplify your message. Repeat your message. Simplify it some more. Then repeat it again.
- Get matching usernames for all your social media accounts.
- Purchase and set up www.YourName.com
- Use firstname@yourname.com for your email address rather than your personal idrinkbeer99@yahoo.com address. It appears more professional.
- Make your email signature useful. Include your website and a call to action.
- Start growing an email list today, even if you don't have an explicit use for it yet.
- Start generating insightful content today.
- Learn about SEO, but not too much. If in doubt, focus on producing great stuff regularly. Everything else will work out fine if you do this.
- Remember that fads and platforms come and go. Your website, blog and email list will be here forever. Don't neglect them.
- Write fewer social media posts and more books.
- If you think you are amazing, the chances are that other people will think you are a prat.
- Learn to be happy without needing to spend cash on stuff.
- Spend less than you earn.
- Figure out a system for dealing with your income and expenses, preferably better than the empty beer box under my desk that I toss train tickets and receipts into.
- Think about getting an agent if you hate talking about money, contracts, or self-promotion.
- Don't sign any contracts before someone brainy reads them and negotiates hard for you.
- Think hard about when to work for free and when to decline work that pays poorly.
- Choose integrity over cash or glory every time.
- Just because you and your mates think an idea is excellent does not mean it will sell at scale.
- How will you earn money when you're old, ugly and arthritic?
- Advice from Goethe: 'A great failing: to see yourself as more than you are and to value yourself at less than you are worth.'
- Strive for passive income (AKA 'earning money while you sleep'). Give a talk, and you receive cash in exchange for that hour of your

life. Sell an online course about the same subject, and people can buy it day and night for years to come. Think about how you can earn money while you sleep (or ride your bike).

- Get paid for your expertise, not your time.
- Don't put all your eggs in one basket: diversify. Also – Don't try to do everything: specialise.
- Focus on rare skills. Outsource the rest. Pay someone to do the things you hate or are bad at to buy yourself time to do the things you are good at and enjoy.
- Beware of selling anything that requires buying stock and sorting logistics.
- Here are some business books that helped me get started:
- *A Book About Innocent* – Innocent
- *Anything You Want* – Derek Sivers
- *Company of One* – Paul Jarvis
- *Deep Work* – Cal Newport
- *Do / Purpose* – David Hieatt
- *How to Get Rich* – Felix Dennis
- *Jab, Jab, Jab, Right Hook* – Gary Vaynerchuk
- *Let My People Go Surfing* – Yvon Chouinard
- *Rework* – Jason Fried
- *The 4-Hour Work Week* – Tim Ferriss
- *The $100 Startup* – Chris Guillebeau
- *The Economist Style Guide* – The Economist
- *The Escape Manifesto* – Escape the City
- *The War of Art* – Steven Pressfield
- *The Wealthy Speaker 2.0* – Jane Atkinson
- *Tools of Titans* – Tim Ferriss
- *Tribes* – Seth Godin (plus all his other books and his blog)
- Ask 'why' before 'what' or 'how' or 'how much?'
- Remember the people that gave you a leg up along the way. Give other folk a hand when you can.
- Read self-help and productivity books, put them into action, then stop reading them and start doing.
- Think differently.
- Remember to enjoy all this. You have chosen to become a Working Adventurer rather than a banker for a reason.
- Be clear about your motives.

- Your working life is long. Allow your pace to ebb and flow, otherwise you will burn out. Fallow times are not wasted times.
- Simplify your message. I began with all sorts of convoluted messages and ideas. Only once I distilled matters down to something as small as 'Sleep on a hill' or the 'the Doorstep Mile' did I start to gain traction.
- Make your story interesting. The world of expeditions is often dull. 'Base Camp was reached at 1700 hours. Dinner was cooked and eaten.' Try to make your adventure stories honest, relevant and accessible.
- An audience responds better if your photos are good, your words are crisp, and your videos are slick. Make your social media updates personable and be available to answer questions (even if only from your shed).
- Give your audience something concrete to do. Loads of folk know deep down that they want to bust out of town and howl at the moon. But they are busy. They are scared. They are embarrassed. They need someone to say, 'Next weekend is the summer solstice. Go and sleep on a hill.' Once it is quantifiable, simple and in the diary, then more people become galvanised to action.
- Remember that this is the entertainment industry.
- Decide whether to be a specialist or a generalist (in your adventures and your output). Both have merit if done well.
- Allow yourself to evolve. What feels like living adventurously now might not fit with your life in a decade. That's OK.
- Be frugal with your plans and ambitious with your goals.
- When you start, nobody knows who you are. Nobody cares about you. Nobody has any inclination to pay you. You need to change this. Think of a way. (My approach was to aim for an exciting project a year, a book a year, and to regard blogging as a 'half time' job – writing several blog posts a week, every week, for years.)
- Make growing an audience of 1000 True Fans your priority. Use this principle as your guiding star in everything you do.
- Save, store and tag your photos. This is boring but helpful. I use Flickr, but you might prefer a different platform. I now have tens of thousands of images, tagged usefully, available at my fingertips.

- Work hard at developing new skills and improving existing skills. In my case, this included: Reading lots to get better at writing and giving talks to get better at speaking. Learning photography to help improve my talks and videography to branch out my story-telling. Researching how to make podcasts and how to build and grow a newsletter series.
- If this is to become your job, you need to treat it as a job. Be prepared to spend more hours behind a computer than up a hill. Or, if not that, work hard to get yourself in a position where this need not be the case.
- Minimise pointless meetings. Try to turn a meeting into a phone call into a five-minute phone call into a five-line email. Then go and ride your bike.
- Help other adventurers with their plans. Celebrate them, don't envy them. It is not a zero-sum game.
- Try to find mentors. Seek out good, clever, motivated, kind, different, humorous individuals to work with.
- Decide upon the boundaries between your private and public lives.
- Read widely. How do other individuals, brands, businesses, organisations make good stuff happen?
- Work harder than everyone else. Remember also that you got into this life because you wanted to spend time in the hills. When the sun shines, go and swim in the river without guilt.
- Be generous with your time, skills, network and expertise. But also – Guard your time.
- Keep as many decisions in your own control as possible.
- Lead, don't follow.
- Write down now what success means to you. Refer to that when you find yourself endlessly chasing the rainbow's end.
- Remember that how you spend your days is how you spend your life.
- People will assume you are lazy. People will think you are rich. People will imagine you are living off handouts.
- Learn what you are good at and what you love. If this intersects with a way to earn money, do it. Learn what sucks your soul dry. As soon as you are able, stop doing these things.
- Keep evolving. Don't be afraid to reinvent yourself.
- There are many ways to lead a tribe. I am happy to sit in my shed by

myself, putting stuff online to grow a community. You might not do it that way. Think hard about what works personally for you.

- Challenge convention and do something different. Find a problem in the world and address it. Answer a question or need in people's lives.
- Make the acquaintance of (and hopefully then the friendship of) other Working Adventurers. I wish I had overcome my shyness and reached out to make more friends at events where adventurers gather.
- Be more excited about opportunities than afraid of making mistakes.
- Take your time to gain experience, learn skills and earn qualifications.
- Don't be a dick.
- Don't miss deadlines.
- Be yourself.
- Don't chase the short-term wins. Be in it for the long haul.
- You don't need advice. Enjoy making your own path.

WHAT WAS YOUR FIRST JOB?

Before leaving school, I worked in my dad's chocolate shop, a local ice cream van, and as a security guard in a gift shop.

Choices

The path I started down as a stimulating pastime 25 years ago has turned into the way I pay for my mortgage and save for my pension. It seems hard to believe sometimes.

Adventure requires a suspension of disbelief, like sport or the square root of -1. Adventure does not matter much, but I have pursued it, pretending that it does as a way to get to what really does matter: purpose, time, health and freedom.

The paradox is interesting. Adventure suggests a carefree lifestyle which I cherish, but at the same time, I take my work seriously. It is a solitary job that depends upon a community and an audience. I try to speak with authority to audiences about their lives whilst being full of doubt about my own life. I've poured so much of my life into adventure, yet I am very aware that it's not a matter of life and death.

Writing this book, I realised that a few principles are repeated over and over in my version of being a Working Adventurer:

- Go on adventures that resonate with you.
- Remember that everyone starts from zero. Begin there and be willing to stick at it for the long haul.
- Become an authority in your niche. Listen to your audience and solve a problem for them.
- Educate, entertain or inspire. Tell your stories to try to bring about some positive change.

Building a life and a career from adventure has been an exercise in persistence and repetition, but also evolution. One privilege of my work is that it has been free to evolve as my life has shifted and unfolded.

In the beginning, I targeted doing what I wanted to do with my days and then figured out a way to make that pay, rather than chasing money first and fitting what I loved in around the edges. Put the large stones of your life into the jar first. The few occasions I have felt disgruntled in my work are when I have prioritised earnings or ego. The times where I have been more successful have been when

I have been at the front of an idea, looking to set the trend rather than follow one. Either that or when I have thought, 'This idea is ridiculous and won't interest anyone else, but it feels irresistible to me, so I am going to do it anyway.' Working on creative work is very satisfying. It has been a lot of fun and personally fulfilling (and hopefully occasionally mildly helpful to others).

I hope that you might have found some parallels with your own work and perhaps found some helpful ideas, or at least the reassurance that you are already doing a better job than me.

Those who have done better than me as a Working Adventurer (in my subjective opinion) have generally done so because they focused and specialised in one thing and became brilliant at it. My fondness for being a generalist has spread me thin by comparison. On the other hand, those who have fared worse than me (in my bitchy, boastful opinion) have worked less hard, not told their stories so well or focused less on the whole package of being a Working Adventurer. Whichever way you look at it, success comes from focusing, persisting and becoming an expert at something that others are not. That does not even touch on the calibre of anyone's actual adventures. Being a Working Adventurer is more about what goes on beneath the shiny tip of the adventure iceberg. Those things are no worse than the adventure; they are just entirely separate – surprisingly separate, perhaps.

This, of course, raises the question of what 'success' means as a Working Adventurer. It is such an individual thing that so long as each person meets their own criteria, they have succeeded. Success for me is to have built a viable career out of doing what I love every day. *Ask An Adventurer* has not been a guidebook or a perfect map. It is just the meandering path that I took and continue to walk down. I am as excited as ever to discover what awaits over the horizon.

Whether you are considering becoming a Working Adventurer yourself, beginning a different sort of self-employed creative work or simply looking to live a little more adventurously, I'd urge you to be bold. Above my desk, I have a quote from author Paulo Coelho that reminds me not to hang about: 'One day or Day One. You decide.'

Begin what you dream of today, with whatever tiny action you can manage. Repeat and grow those small actions until they become habits, and you will build momentum and confidence.

One of my earliest adventure heroes, Wilfred Thesiger, called his autobiography *The Life of my Choice*. I am so grateful for how my working life has unfolded. I'm writing this in a shed I love, paid for by a book I enjoyed writing. I am drinking coffee, listening to music and enjoying the goldfinches squabbling outside in the sunshine. When I finish jotting these last lines, I am going to open the map that's sitting on my desk and start planning my next adventure. By the time you read these lines, I'll be out on my bike again, taking photos, scribbling notes and coming up with a new book idea. And I get to call all this work. I am a lucky man.

Here are some other ways you can follow what I do:

- Sign up for my newsletters: www.AlastairHumphreys.com/newsletters
- Listen to my podcasts: www.AlastairHumphreys.com/podcasts
- Follow on me on social media: @al_humphreys on Instagram and Twitter, 'Alastair Humphreys' on Facebook and YouTube
- Read my other books, including several for children: www.AlastairHumphreys.com/shop
- Listen to my audiobooks: search 'Alastair Humphreys Audible'

If you have enjoyed this book, please leave a quick review on Amazon (search 'Amazon Ask An Adventurer') or post a photo of the book on social media to tell your friends about it. These things all make a massive difference to the success of a book. Thank you.

Acknowledgements

Thank you to everyone who has gone before me and taught me so much about every aspect of being a Working Adventurer through your books, blogs and podcasts. Your generosity in sharing your skills and expertise encouraged me to go ahead with this book and toss my two penn'orths of experience into the ring.

A sincere thank you to my agents Caroline Rose, Jessica Woollard and Jo Cantello. You have done so much to turn my enthusiastic adventuring into a viable way of life. I really appreciate all your hard work, advice and patience.

Thank you to the teams at Eye Books, Harper Collins and Bonnier Books for your support over the years, as well as to the machines at Amazon's KDP programme.

Thank you for editing help to David Charles, Jon Doolan, Rosie Watson, Paul Deegan, Rob Bushby, Anna McNuff, Corleen Gallinger and Andy McFetrich. Thank you to DJ Format and Abdominal for allowing me to quote their lyrics.

Thank you to Jim Shannon (www.JShannon.com) and Anna Brones (www.AnnaBrones.com) for the book design and front cover.

And a huge thank you to everyone who asked the questions that became this book. Thank you for your interest and support.

About the author

Alastair Humphreys is a British Adventurer and Author. He spent four years cycling round the world, a journey of 46,000 miles through 60 countries and five continents.

More recently Alastair has walked across southern India, rowed across the Atlantic Ocean, run six marathons through the Sahara desert, completed a crossing of Iceland, busked through Spain and participated in an expedition in the Arctic, close to the magnetic North Pole. He has trekked 1000 miles across the Empty Quarter desert and 120 miles round the M25 – one of his pioneering microadventures. He was named as one of National Geographic's Adventurers of the year for 2012. This is his 13th book.

Other Books by Alastair Humphreys

1. *Moods of Future Joys.* Cycling from England to South Africa. *I think all authors are secretly appalled and proud of their first published book.*

2. *Thunder and Sunshine.* Cycling the rest of the way around the world. *Better written than book 1, and far more pages per pound.*

3. *Ten Lessons from the Road.* Some life lessons gleaned along the way. *Someone recently taught me to be kind to my younger self, which has helped me be more fond of this simple book.*

4. *The Boy Who Biked The World. Part 1: cycling from England to South Africa,* written for kids. *Every email I get saying, "my child hated reading until they picked this book up", makes four years of saddlesore feel worthwhile.*

5. *The Boy Who Biked The World. Part 2: cycling from Patagonia to Alaska,* written for kids.

6. *The Boy Who Biked The World. Part 3: cycling from Siberia to England,* written for kids.

7. *There Are Other Rivers.* Walking alone across southern India. *A pig-headed, honest experimentation with going it alone in publishing. This book is flawed, but I'm proud of it.*

8. *Microadventures.* A guidebook to short, simple, local adventures. *This book is the one that will be mentioned if I ever earn an obituary in the Little Puddledown Gazette.*

9. *Grand Adventures.* A guidebook for big, bold, epic adventures. *This book has sold spectacularly few copies. But if you're dreaming of a whopping adventure, it could just tip you into action.*

10. *Great Adventurers.* The adventurers who inspired me to action, written for kids. *My most successful book in terms of translations, and my only award-winning book.*

11. *My Midsummer Morning.* Busking badly through Spain. *Depending on where you are in your life, this is either a daft adventure, a mid-life crisis, or a beacon of hope. The book I am most proud of writing.*

12. *The Doorstep Mile.* A self-help book to turn big ideas into tiny actions. *Depending on where you are in life, this book will either make you vomit, cringe, or perhaps change your life. I'm willing to endure the first two for the few who might actually take action.*

13. *A Notebook for Living Adventurously*. Listeners to the Living Adventurously podcast enjoy the question cards about finding a balance between work and play, the barriers that stop us doing what we dream of, how we overcome fears, and where you sit on a scale of weirdness from 1 to 10… *The questions from the cards are laid out as writing prompts in this notebook. Answer each one thoroughly and you will be well on the way to writing the backstory to your autobiography as well as planning the next decade of your life!*
14. *A Notebook for Everyday Adventures*. A cheap and cheerful notebook designed to help you answer the questions raised in *The Doorstep Mile* and begin living more adventurously today.